A SEMINAL WORK IN THE STUDY OF ISLAMIC BELIEFS

FOREWORD BY DR. SAJJAD RIZVI

DIVINE
LEADERSHIP

A RATIONAL APPROACH

H.E. AYATOLLAH

SAYYID JAFAR ALHAKEEM

SEMINARY PROFESSOR OF ISLAMIC SCIENCES

COMPILED BY MOHAMED ALI ALBODAIRI

THE MAINSTAY FOUNDATION

Author: Ayatollah Sayyid Jafar Al-Hakeem

Foreword by: Dr. Sajjad H. Rizvi

Compiled by: Mohamed Ali Albodairi

Printed in the United States.

ISBN: 978-1943393466

To the seal of what came before.
To the herald of what was to come.
To the master over it all.
To our beloved Holy Prophet Muḥammad (s).

CONTENTS

Note on Usage and Spelling ... *ix*
About the Author ... *xi*
Foreword ... *xiii*
Compiler's Preface ... *xvii*

Introduction ... 1

Theoretical Framework ... 7
Foundational Context ... 9
Conceptual Framework ... 23
Conceptual Corollaries ... 33
Qur'anic Framework ... 43
On Knowledge and Authority ... 53
On Religious Authority ... 67

Practical Implications ... 81
On Naṣṣ ... 83
Between Naṣṣ and Reason ... 93
Our Responsibility ... 113
Tawallī and Tabarrī ... 127

Addressing Misconceptions ... 145
On Authority ... 147
On Immaculacy and the Holy Qur'an ... 155
On Immaculacy and Free Will ... 167
Epilogue ... 173

Referenced Works ... *177*

NOTE ON USAGE AND SPELLING

We have chosen to standardize usage and spelling in a manner that should be accessible to most readers.

Words that are commonly used in the English language or are defined in a standard English dictionary are used in their common spelling (e.g. Mecca, not Makkah). This applies to some commonly used given names (e.g. Ali, not ʿAli). This is also specifically applied to the word Shia (not Shiʿah).

Diacritical marks have been omitted, except for the *hamza* (ʾ) and the *ʿayn* (ʿ). We have used the IJMES transliteration system, with some notable deviations. For the ninth Arabic letter *thal*, we have opted to use th (like the th in *that*). The Arabic *ta marbutah* is rendered *ah* if it is not in the Arabic *idafah* construction. If it is in an *idafah* construction, it is rendered *at* except where it is part of a given name.

All words are rendered in their *marfu*ʿ state where possible (e.g. Ali ibn Abu Talib, not Ali ibn Abi Talib).

Elision are rendered only if the elided letter is preceded by a *harf ʿillah* (e.g. Thu'l-Hijjah). A notable exception is found in all given names beginning in *ʿAbd*, which are always elided with the succeeding name (i.e. ʿAbdulmalik, not ʿAbd al-Malik).

The reader should note that the supplication of *salawat* (may God send his peace and blessings upon Muhammad and the household of Muhammad) and salutations (peace be upon them) are usually recited at the mention of the Holy Prophet and his family. This is normally marked in elaborate calligraphy in Arabic text, or with (s), (a), or a similar mark in English text. Such marks do not appear in this book so as not to disturb the flow of the reader. At times, we have also dropped the title of some important religious and historical figures. For example, we refer sometimes to Ali rather than Imam Ali. Again, the intent in these instances is to maintain the flow of the book. These decisions in no way are meant to disregard the status and reverence of these individuals.

Finally, we relied on the translation of Ali Quli Qaraʾi when citing to the verses of the Holy Qurʾan throughout this book, with minor adaptations that allowed us to weave the verses more properly with the rest of the work.

ABOUT THE AUTHOR

His Eminence Ayatollah Sayyid Jafar al-Hakeem is a prominent professor and public intellectual at the Islamic Seminary (*al-ḥawza al-ʿilmiyya*) in the shrine city of Najaf in Iraq. Born in 1965 to a prominent scholarly family, Sayyid al-Hakeem began his seminary studies at the age of 12.

On May 10, 1983, Sayyid al-Hakeem was arrested and detained along with his father Ayatollah ʿAbdulṣāḥib al-Hakeem and over 60 other members of his family by the regime of Saddam Hussein. Less than two weeks after the arrest, the author's father and other members of the family were executed without any criminal charges or trial. The remainder of the family would continue to suffer torture in the prisons of the Saddam regime.

Despite the circumstances, Sayyid al-Hakeem and the remainder of his family would continue their religious studies from within Saddam's dark cells. No books were allowed in Saddam's prisons, but being imprisoned alongside so many prominent religious scholars allowed for the continuation of classes and study circles.

After more than seven years of imprisonment, Sayyid al-Hakeem and a small group of cellmates were able to escape imprisonment and flee to Iran. There, Sayyid al-Hakeem joined the Islamic Seminary of Qum, where he studied under the tutelage of scholars such as Ayatollah Sayyid Taqī al-Qummī (d. 2016) and Ayatollah Shaykh Muḥammad al-Sanad.

After the fall of the Saddam regime in 2003, Sayyid al-Hakeem returned to the holy city of Najaf to rejoin its seminary. He currently teaches advanced seminars (*baḥth khārij*) in *fiqh* and *uṣūl*, as well as seminars in epistemology, philosophy, theosophy, and theology.

In addition to his scholarly work, Sayyid al-Hakeem is a prominent Iraqi public intellectual. He appeared as a witness in the trial of Saddam, testifying to the cruel sectarian persecution of Shia scholars and scholarly families. He often speaks on issues of religious identity, pluralism, civic engagement, and contemporary issues. Sayyid al-Hakeem has visited the United States and Europe, where he had the opportunity to address and discuss these topics with both Muslim and non-Muslim audiences.

FOREWORD

There is little doubt that the defining theological feature of Shiʿi Islam is the centrality of the Imamate as both the succession to the prophetic function and the continuity of divine guidance for humanity until the end of times. The imamate thus acts both as the face of divine agency in the cosmos and reflects humanity, acting as the focal mediating force in the cosmos. From early on in the sacred and theological history of the Shiʿi tradition, theologians and philosophers have argued for the absolute requirement of trusting faith in God for humans, for believers, to recognise the Imam of their time and to channel their love and obedience to God through devotion to him. Both scriptural proofs and rational arguments have been adduced in favour of the position. For the latter, from at least the time of al-Shaykh al-Mufīd (d. 1022) and al-Sharīf al-Murtaḍā (d. 1044), we have the famous syllogistic argument for the necessity of the Imamate. The first syllogism follows this line: Justice (*al-ʿadl*) is the absolute and superabundantly central property of God; Justice entails that God cannot place a burden on humans that they cannot bear (*taklīf mā lā yuṭāq*); therefore, Justice entails that God provide humans with facilitating acts of grace (*alṭāf*) in order to fulfil their duties, reciprocity, and need to 'thank the benefactor' (*shukr al-munʿim*). Thus, we find justice and its activity through grace are central to the divine economy and providence. Consequently, we have the additional syllogism: God must necessarily provide acts of facilitating grace to assist humans; the imamate is an expression of God's facilitating grace; therefore, the imamate is necessary.

It is a pleasure to write these few words about this thoughtful book by one of the leading teachers of the seminary in Najaf and public theologians of the Shiʿi tradition, Sayyid Jaʿfar al-Hakeem, scion of an eminent scholarly family of the seminary whose contribution to learning and ethical formation has been central to modern history. This book is a worthy contribution to our contemporary understanding of the need for the imamate as a lasting link and connection to the divine, as an unfolding of divine providence and as a helping hand and act of grace that takes us back to the loving embrace of the divine. Consistent with some important elements of the 'new theology' (*kalām jadīd*) of the modern Shiʿi period, Sayyid Jaʿfar does not focus on the polemics that have often characterised discussions of the imamate in the tradition (although he does not shy away from presenting robustly the Twelver Shiʿi position). Rather, he places his arguments within a broader metaphysical framework that complements the close reading of scriptural texts. Consistent with the medieval tradition of Khwāja Naṣīr al-Dīn Ṭūsī and ʿAllāma al-Ḥillī, he brings those scriptural proofs, reading of the Qurʾan and the hadith of the Prophet and his progeny, into conversation with a metaphysical vision of the unfolding of divine providence. Imamate is necessary because God is necessary. A metaphysical order entails the existence of the proof of God and His remnant in the cosmos; similarly, the proper functioning of a moral order requires us to recognise the source of all value lies in God and his friends and intimate ones. This is precisely why Sayyid Jaʿfar links the necessity of the Imam to the human desire to perfect oneself, to fulfil and complete our pure and practical intellects and their activity.

A fuller understanding of the political theology of the Shiʿi tradition – which is very much a desideratum of our times – requires us to understand the modes in which divine justice and sovereignty are manifest in our world. This is the notion and indeed the reality of the Imamate. Sayyid Jaʿfar shows us how the metaphysics of the existence of God and of the Imam are not just mere notions, beings of reason without much practical need or reality, but in fact expressions and explanations of metaphysical truths that pertain and intervene in human life and human history. I would like to thank and commend the Mainstay Foundation, those who compiled and transcribed this work, and those brought it to its fruition as a publication for their contribution. One can but pray that this work will be fruitfully read by those within the Shiʿi community as well as those outside of it who want to understand why the presence and existence of the Imam is so important for this significant sector of the Muslim community and the brotherhood of humanity globally.

Sayyid Sajjad H. Rizvi[1]
London

[1] Dr. Sayyid Sajjad Rizvi is Associate Professor of Islamic Intellectual History and Director of the Centre for the Study of Islam at the University of Exeter in the United Kingdom.

COMPILER'S PREFACE

The concepts of monotheistic faith (*tawḥīd*) and divinely designated prophecy (*nubuwwah*) are foundational principles of faith to which all Muslims assent. They are embodied in the expression of the two testimonies (*shahādatān*) – that there is no god but God and that Muḥammad is the messenger of God. Yet even though all Muslims adhere to these principles, there is a wide range of disagreement as to the intricate details.

The topic of divine leadership (*imamate*) is integral to the Shia creed, second only to tawḥīd and nubuwwah. Part of its significance – as the reader will come to find – comes from its establishment of a divinely appointed and immaculate religious authority. We go back to these immaculate authorities (imams) for guidance not only on matters of religious practice, but to better understand the specifics of Islam's foundational concepts and theology. It is therefore an essential doctrine in our attempt to understand our faith.

It is this understanding of imamate as an integral and foundational concept that compelled us to undertake the task of compiling and publishing this treatise. Our aim is to provide the reader with a comprehensive and concrete understanding of the subject that will contribute to a richer and deeper understanding of tawḥīd and nubuwwah.

This treatise is based on a set of thirty lectures delivered by His Eminence Ayatollah Sayyid Jafar al-Hakeem to a group of students. The lectures came about as a supplement to the normal course of study, in which Sayyid al-Hakeem was discussing the text of *Sharḥ Tajrīd al-I'tiqād (Kashf al-murād)* by Jamāl al-Dīn Ibn al-Muṭahhar al-Ḥillī (d. 726/1325), a central school-text in the seminary for studying Shia theology. Seeing that the text did not cover the topic in a sufficient manner for the contemporary age, he put the book aside and set out to draw a theoretical framework for the topic of imamate in a detailed and novel way.

I have personally benefit from Sayyid al-Hakeem's immense knowledge, wisdom, and insight. Whether it was in his trips to the United States or in my trips to Iraq, I always had the blessing of meeting him and being at his service. His insights always showed a novel perspective on any issue. His thoughts on imamate specifically has a profound impact on me personally and spiritually.

Upon the suggestion of some of Sayyid al-Hakeem's students, the Mainstay Foundation undertook the task of compiling these lectures for an English-speaking audience. The purpose is to shed new light on the Shia understanding of imamate and its practical implications, as well as answering prevalent questions and misconceptions.

We hope that we were able to deliver to our reader an insightful book that will bolster their understanding of imamate and strengthen their relationship with the immaculate leaders of the Holy Household (*ahl al-bayt*).

Finally, we want to take this opportunity to thank you for your support. As students of Islam and as compilers of this text, our greatest purpose is to please God by passing along these teachings to others. By picking up this book, you have lent your crucial support in this endeavor. We hope that you will continue your support throughout the rest of this book, and we ask that you keep us in your prayers whenever you pick it up.

Mohamed Ali Albodairi[1]

---

[1] Mohamed Ali Albodairi is a researcher, author, translator, and attorney at law. He is the author of numerous books on history and theology, including *Understanding Karbala* (abridged and adapted from the original work of HE Grand Ayatollah Muhammad Saeed al-Hakeem).

INTRODUCTION

In the name of God, the Most Beneficent, the Most Merciful

The topic of imamate (*imamate*), or divine leadership, is one of great significance within the Muslim worldview. The topic is so seminal that entire schools of thought were built and distinguished based on their differing views on the subject. It is the theme of countless Qur'anic verses and prophetic traditions.

Despite its great importance, imamate was not always afforded its proper attention and explanation. The imams from the progeny of the Holy Prophet taught their companions the unequivocal significance of imamate, including many supplications that incorporated a great deal of reverence for it. They placed great emphasis on rituals of reverence and devotion, such as visitation of their tombs (performing *ziyārah*) – especially the shrine of Imam al-Ḥusayn.

Still, we find that some of the imams' close companions did not fully appreciate the magnitude of the issue. One such companion was so struck by Imam al-Ṣādiq's prayer for the visitors of Imam al-Ḥusayn that he confessed to the Imam, "By God, I wish I would have visited him instead of performing Ḥajj!"[1]

Thanks to the work of our imams and the dedication of our scholars, we have made strides in our understanding of the subject. The gravity of Imam al-Ḥusayn's mission and sacrifice is so engrained in the hearts and

[1] al-Qummī, *Kāmil al-ziyārāt*, 228-229.

minds of his followers that visiting his shrine has become an intuitive part of religious life.

Still, there is much work ahead of us. The concept and its practical implications are still unclear in the minds of many of the followers of the Holy Household. This lack of clarity permeates into the questions and misconceptions that we hear in public discourse.

This treatise is an attempt to contribute to the development of our understanding of the topic. It is an attempt to clarify seminal concepts and answer lingering questions.

In addressing these complex topics, philosophers often take one of two approaches. The first approach is to tackle these questions with an eye to demonstrative arguments and proofs; setting out premises and deriving conclusions in a formulaic manner. This is the approach of many Muslim philosophers.

A second approach is to present a philosophical framework with clear thought and impeccable internal consistency. With this approach, the philosopher paints a vibrant and harmonious picture, allowing the reader to see the beauty of its conclusions. The demonstrative proofs are still present, but given a supportive role that complements a clearly articulated conceptual picture.

This treatise will use the second approach in establishing its premises and conclusions. We will not provide exhaustive demonstrative proofs for the concepts and understandings presented here. Instead, we will emphasize the beauty and internal consistency of our philosophical understanding of imamate.

* * *

This treatise will do three things: set out a theoretical framework, outline the practical implications, and answer some misconceptions regarding the topic of imamate. As such, the book is divided into three parts.

In the first part, we will provide a theoretical framework for our understanding of imamate in light of reason and revelation.

We will begin by establishing a foundational context for understanding imamate. We will provide a perspective on the purpose of human creation and the role of religion in human life. We will then look at the historic Muslim debate over imamate as a means of highlighting the importance of these topics.

Next, we will provide a general explanation of imamate according to the school of the Holy Household of the Prophet (*ahl al-bayt*). We will first address the linguistic meanings of imamate as a starting point for our discussion. We will then explain the theoretical and practical rational foundations of our conception of imamate.

Having provided a conceptual foundation, the next chapter will provide eight conceptual corollaries that follow from such an explanation.

We will then delve into the Qur'anic framework of the concept of imamate. We will see that the Holy Qur'an focuses on and explains the concept of imamate in detail. It establishes the concept as a constant in the realm of creation and links it directly with the divine realm.

We will then turn to study the link between knowledge and authority. We will see that imamate is built upon an individual's attainment of a particular knowledge, of special quantity and quality.[2] This knowledge qualifies the imam to hold the highest position of authority in the created realm.

Our discussion will then focus on the imams' religious authority. We will attempt to understand their role as leaders in light of their enemies' campaign to remove them from the public sphere. We will see how they focused their efforts on the building of a righteous community within Muslim society.

The second part of this treatise will outline a number of practical conceptions and implications that follow our understanding of imamate.

We will first look at the concept of designation (*naṣṣ*) and its practical implications. We will clarify why we believe that naṣṣ is necessary and why its alternative is insufficient. We will lay out our conception of what naṣṣ entails and its relationship to rational evidence. This discussion will lead us to understand four practical advantages to holding to the doctrine of naṣṣ.

We will then turn to address the responsibilities dictated by our understanding of imamate. We will begin by addressing the relationship between the concepts of imamate and *tawḥīd* – namely the intricate correlation between the two concepts found in the Holy Qur'an and the noble traditions. We will see that the depth and reality of tawḥīd comes with a proper understanding, acceptance, and adherence to imamate. We will

---

[2] The imams' particular knowledge is discussed in detail in Chapter 5 *On Knowledge and Authority*.

address the centrality of faith to human experience and understanding of the world, and the integral role of the concept and reality of imamate within that vision. With that, we hope to address a misconception that some may have regarding the practicality of these discussions.

Next, we will turn to the concepts of *tawallī* and *tabarrī*.[3] We will see that the idea of tawallī places a number of practical responsibilities by which each believer ought to abide. It is a concept much broader than political support and affiliation. Tawallī is not only an affection and love that we hold towards the Holy Household, but an obligation to follow, remember, and revere them. We will also see that tabarrī is a natural outcome of tawallī, the two concepts being opposite sides of a single coin. Just as tawallī dictates love and adherence to the Holy Household, tabarrī dictates repudiation of their enemies. These concepts must be understood within their proper scope and application.

In the third part of the book, we will address some common misconceptions about imamate and its role in the Muslim worldview.

First, we will look at the misconception that our belief in imamate is at odds with the concept of tawḥīd. Throughout history, there were those who aimed to discredit our school of thought by describing our conception of imamate as heretical and violating monotheism. We will provide a set of counterarguments that outline the fallacy of such presumptions. We will also outline the conceptual framework that allows us to make sense of our understanding of God's infinite nature and the authority which He gave to His select servants.

We will then look at the misconception that the Holy Qurʾan is incompatible with the concept of immaculacy (*ʿiṣma*).[4] The claim is that the Holy Book contains many verses that chastise and admonish the prophets and messengers, showing that they are fallible human beings. We will refute this misconception by first providing some guiding insights on the Holy Qurʾan and how it should be approached from an evidentiary standpoint. We will then provide a number of answers to the

---

[3] Respectively, devoted adherence to and love for the Holy Prophet and his Immaculate household, and disavowal and repudiation of the enemies of the Holy Prophet and his Immaculate household.

[4] Twelver Shia Muslims believe that prophets and Imams are granted a 'blessing such that they have no occasion to disobey a command or commit a sin, despite their ability to do so' - see Ibn al-Muṭahhar al-Ḥillī, *al-Bāb al-ḥādī ʿashar*, 41–42. They are capable of sinning, but they choose not to act on that capacity. This quality is what we refer to as their 'immaculate nature.'

misconception by analyzing Muslims' unanimous belief in immaculacy, studying the Qur'anic basis for that belief, and outlining a model for understanding the verses that seem to contradict with our proposed framework.

Finally, we will address the misconception of immaculacy's incompatibility with the idea of free will. We will lay out an understanding of how the prophets, messengers, and imams were chosen for those roles. We will see that the choice was based on God's knowledge of each individual's will and capacity. We will point out that – although our understanding of the wisdom behind the particulars of creation may not be complete – there is a way to reconcile our conception of imamate and immaculacy with our belief in mankind's free will.

PART I
THEORETICAL FRAMEWORK

FOUNDATIONAL CONTEXT

The elements of our universe are not disconnected, where every being is completely and absolutely distinct from all others. There are similarities and commonalities that bring things together, as well as distinctions that separate different elements in existence. This creates sets and subsets of things that can be observed and analyzed.

Existence (*al-wujūd*) is one common thread that runs throughout the world. We observe everything around us – every entity – and we see that it exists. Existence is both the principle of commonality and of differentiation; it itself is what brings everything together and separates what is from what is not.[1]

Yet when we observe existence, we see that it comes in different forms. We see that there are distinct entities that make up the realm of existence. And each of these entities has certain characteristics that set it apart from every other entity. Each has its distinct identity. These divergent characteristics are what allow us to observe and make sense of this universe.

For us to identify each entity, we must therefore look at both the similarities that it shares with all others, as well as the distinctions that separate it from them. We start with existence, which separates every

[1] This, of course, is a reference to the metaphysical principle in the philosophy of Ṣadr al-Dīn Shīrāzī known as Mullā Ṣadrā (d. 1045/1636) known as the ontological priority and modulation of existence (*aṣālat al-wujūd wa-tashkīk al-wujūd*). See ʿAllāma Ṭabāṭabāʾī, *The Elements of Islamic Metaphysics*, 7–14.

existent thing from the abyss of non-existence. Existence within our observable cosmos is divided into the mental, the extra-mental (or physical or concrete), and metaphysical. The ability to grow and develop unites all living things and distinguishes them from inanimate objects. The ability to move freely separates animals from other living organisms.

Distinction of Humanity

Among these entities, humanity holds a special place. The distinctive characteristics for every other species of living or nonliving entities cannot compare to the distinctive qualities of humanity. Although we are animals by nature – we move, eat, rest, and grow – our distinctive human qualities give us an advantage over others. Our humanity allowed us to establish dominion over the realm of nature and its beasts. It drives us to either protect and nurture or abuse and exploit that dominion.

Biologically speaking, we are animals without much distinction from all other animals. What separates humans from horses? Both are species of the animal kingdom. Both are classified as mammals. Each has its scientific classification of order, family, and genus. Horses are classified into a species (Equus ferus) that distinguishes them biologically from other animals, like llamas or rhinoceros. Humans are also classified as a species (Homo sapiens) that separates us from horses and sheep.

Yet our human distinction has allowed us to dominate all other species. Although we may share the same rank in terms of biological classification, our distinctive characteristics not only differentiate us from all others, but they also grant us privilege over them. Our human characteristics allow us to be dominant over the horse and make it subservient to our needs. Our ingenuity has even allowed us to make engines out of inanimate steel – engines that are more useful to us than horses.

This may not have been true historically. In the early stages of our history, humanity did not possess the ability to dominate and domesticate other animal species. Our human qualities allowed us to evolve so rapidly over such a small period of time – relatively speaking – that we began to govern our environment and harness it as we pleased.

What is it that distinguishes humanity, making it so different from all other beings we observe around us? What is it that makes us 'human'?

Philosophers often name two distinctly human qualities that allowed us to be dominant – free will and reason. These two attributes allowed humanity to move out of the slow pace of advancement that all other living entities experience. They allowed humanity to advance exponentially, developing the skills and knowledge that allow us to dominate so effectively.

Movement is in humanity's very nature. We as a species cannot stop and rest. We continually seek advancements, to better our lives. If we wish to compile our understanding of human nature – as studied in the sciences of philosophy, theology, and ethics – the best analogy that we can draw is to that of a rock climber that will not and cannot stop. There is constant movement toward higher and higher levels, with the constant threat of falling down an endless abyss.

Ethics allows us to understand what it means for us humans to either ascend or descend. Reason and free will alone do not entail that our movements are always for the better. Our reason may lead us to understand the workings of subatomic particles. Our determination may lead to the industrialization of the globe. But these advancements do not mean that we are on the ascent if they lunge us into a global arms race or catastrophic climate change.

Our intelligence may be the distinguishing factor that sets us apart from all other animals. Yet, we cannot perceive this advantage as a merit if it is not directed properly and utilized correctly. Our reason allows us to more effectively satisfy our appetites. But what merit or distinction does that give us? And if we allow ourselves to pursue these appetites without inhibition, are we not worse than all other animals that do not have the gift of reason?

Role of Religion

So, what role does religion play in this worldview? Religion is the rope that helps the climber ascend the heights of this mountain. It is the guide that ensures we continue to ascend towards the better, and not fall into degradation and deviance.

This does not mean that religion supplants any of the other human faculties and achievements. Religion does not ask us to discard reason. It does not inhibit us from making advances in science. It does not foreclose on human ingenuity in industry and commerce. Rather, it directs our growth so that we are growing for the better. In other words, religion provides the moral framework, fine-tuning our moral compass, for human growth in light of our distinctly human characteristics.

Moreover, religion provides the framework of proper interaction between members of the human species. Our human qualities not only allowed us to dominate nature but drove us towards domination of one another. Our human qualities lead to complex social, political, and economic systems that define the boundaries of our group interactions. They also lead to strife, war, and devastation unparalleled in the animal kingdom.

Religion did not come to displace humanity's achievements. It came to regulate it to differing degrees based on the subject matter. This can most explicitly be seen in Islam's treatment of transactional issues. Prior to the Holy Prophet Muḥammad delivering the message of Islam in Arabia, people dealt with one another in accordance with a set of rational rules. They understood that two individuals may enter into a contract upon mutual assent, signified by an offer and an acceptance. They had particular rules that governed sharecropping arrangements. People entered into business partnerships and made investments in one another's businesses. Islam did not supplant any of that. Rather, it ratified all these sorts of relationships with a degree of regulation. The most overt of these regulations was the prohibition of usury. God says in the Holy Qur'an,

قَالُوا إِنَّمَا الْبَيْعُ مِثْلُ الرِّبَا ۗ وَأَحَلَّ اللَّهُ الْبَيْعَ وَحَرَّمَ الرِّبَا

They say, 'Trade is just like usury.' While Allah has allowed trade and forbidden usury.[2]

Still, disagreements about the role of religion and its teachings were prevalent in the formative years of Islam, as they are today. Differences amongst Muslims lead to various understandings of the faith – and to the creation of multiple confessions and schools of thought. What were the primary factors that drove these disagreements?

THE GREAT SCHISM IN THE FOLD OF ISLAM

Many have characterized the differences between Muslim schools of thought as centered around the issue of identifying the rightful successor to the Holy Prophet Muḥammad. This generally characterizes Muslims as either pro-government or opposition. As the Encyclopedia Britannica puts it, "The division of Islam into two major groups, Sunni and

[2] The Holy Qur'an, 2:275.

Shīʿī, has its origins in the struggles over the proper line of succession to the Prophet Muḥammad."[3]

This simplification and misstatement of the issue has its roots in propaganda that has been used against the followers of the Holy Household since the formative years of Islam. The attempt is to portray Shiʿi Islam as a political movement that rejected the rule of certain personalities and installed its own instead, thus stripping this school of thought of its theological and philosophical value and merit.

To better understand this school of thought, let us first provide a more accurate synopsis of the Muslim debate and schism that unfolded after the passing of the Holy Prophet. We can summarize our view of these differences in the following eight points:

Religious Authority. There is a genuine disagreement over the source of religious authority in Islam. The debate was not only about who would be the legitimate head of the polity, but about the source of religious legitimacy and understanding. Is the king or caliph a divinely endowed representative chosen by divine providence? Or is there a religious authority external to the political system which may conflict with the caliph? The Holy Household had a significant historical presence among the Muslims. They were teachers of the highest caliber, and many of those who later became known as 'Sunni' scholars were their pupils. Yet if you look at the Sunni tradition, you find that they are seldom mentioned or invoked as authorities. Their absence from that sphere is an indication of the intentional attempt to remove them from the attention of the Muslim public. The degree to which the Holy Household is listened to and followed is a major theme of the debate between Muslim schools of thought.

Legitimacy and Continuance. There is a disagreement over the continuance of the phenomenon of imamate after the passing of the Holy Prophet. If you study the school of thought of the majority, you will find a dilemma with respect to the continuance of legitimacy. Where did legitimacy come from after the passing of the Holy Prophet? If it derived from the people, how could one caliph appoint the next? Or how could one appoint a committee and task it with selecting the next caliph? Or how could a caliph seize the throne by force and bequeaths it to his

---

[3] Appleby, R. Scott. *Encyclopaedia Britannica*, "The Sunni-Shiʿite Division Within Islam." Encyclopaedia Britannica, 2008.

descendants? The school of thought of the majority finds legitimacy in all of these scenarios, without a convincing explanation for the source of that legitimacy how it was transferred.[4]

On the other hand, you find that the school of thought of the Holy Household provides a concrete theory for legitimacy and its continuance – what we call designation (naṣṣ).[5] It is through naṣṣ that we believe in imamate of ʿAlī ibn Abī Ṭālib and his qualified descendants, all the way to the imam of our time, the awaited al-Mahdī. Thus, as a natural consequence of this disagreement and its circumstances arose a debate over the idea and possibility of occultation (*al-ghaybah*) – along with its spiritual and intellectual aspects.[6]

Immaculacy and *Ijtihād*. The followers of the Holy Household consider immaculacy a necessity, whereas others do not. This was not merely a theoretical debate. The disagreement over immaculacy resulted in the differences in understanding the process of *ijtihād*. For the followers of the Holy Household, *ijtihād* was always a process subordinate to naṣṣ – a process to understand and apply the words and teachings of the immaculate imams. On the other hand, the school of thought of the majority was compelled to adopt ideas such as *raʾy* (non-scriptural opinion), *qiyās* (analogical reasoning), and *istiṣlāḥ* (consideration of public interest).[7] Foresight of the grave errors that such techniques in ijtihad can

---

[4] Many explanations provided are rooted in the assumption that the early generation of Muslims had clarity and consensus on these issues. Thus, they provided a precedent from which legitimacy followed. The flaws in this worldview are numerous, the most jarring of which is the reality of disagreement amongst that first generation. How can the tragedy and sermons of Lady Fāṭimah, the daughter of the Prophet, be explained as part of a legitimate consensus? How is a consensus even possible in light of the historic political disunity amongst Muslims at that time? Three of the four 'Rightly Guided' caliphs were assassinated. The five years in which Imam ʿAlī ruled were mired in conflict, rebellion, and civil war. These are only a few of the many counterexamples to communal consensus.

[5] *Naṣṣ* (past tense verb): raised, demonstrated. Naṣṣ can properly be understood as 'divine declaration or designation'. The word is so broad that it has been used to denote a multitude of meanings in technical writings. We will address five such meanings in a later chapter. But also see al-Ḥillī, *al-Bāb al-ḥādī ʿashar*, 43–44.

[6] Occultation (*ghaybah*) is the state of the twelfth immaculate Imam according to the Twelver Shia school of thought. In this state, the Imam is not living openly in society – as his grandfathers did. He is not present and available to his followers like his forfathers were, but neither is he completely absent. He is "like the sun behind the clouds," living incognito amongst us. See al-Ḥillī, *al-Bāb al-ḥādī ʿashar*, 52.

[7] *Raʾy* ('opinion' or 'rational discretion'), *qiyās* ('analogical reasoning'), and *istiṣlāḥ* ('consideration of public interest') are tools of jurisprudence used by some Muslim jurists in the process of ijtihad.

reap led to the curtailment of the concept's application. At the same time, the passing of time meant that people became more estranged from the time and aims of the Holy Prophet. This led to 'closing the gates of ijtihad' in the Sunni school of thought after the Four Imams who lived in the first and second century after hijra.[8] Conversely, *ijtihād* continues to be an accepted and systemized practice within Shia Islam.[9] With the rejection of immaculacy, the majoritarian Muslims also faced an issue with identifying the prerequisites of leadership and judging the merits of their leaders. The highlight of that contradiction came with the movement of Imam al-Ḥusayn who declared,

> إنّا أهل بيت النبوّة، ومعدن الرسالة، ومختلف الملائكة، بنا فتح الله، وبنا يختم، ويزيد فاسق فاجر، شارب الخمر، قاتل النفس المحترمة، معلن بالفسق والفجور، ومثلي لا يبايع مثله
>
> *We are the household of the Prophet, the core of the message, and those whom the angels frequent. God presented [His message] through us, and he will seal it with us. Yazīd is a deviant, a miscreant, a drunkard, and a murderer. He has publicly professed his deviance and impiety. Someone like me will never pay allegiance to the likes of him.*[10]

Still, Yazīd and others continue to be respected, with the phrase 'may God be pleased with him' often repeated after any mention of his name. The same is true with many other Muslim leaders who continued in their deviance, while many Muslims refused to judge their legitimacy and merit.

Moreover, the stated rejection of immaculacy carries a hidden contradiction. In lieu of the immaculacy of fourteen individuals, the majority professed the idea of the absolutely probative and righteous nature of

---

[8] 'Closing the gates of ijtihad' is a phrase commonly used to describe the emergence of the four jurisprudential schools in Sunni Islam. Had the gates of ijtihad remained open, there would be room for more schools to emerge. Sunni Islam severely restricted the scope of *ijtihād* with limits that are not set by primary religious sources. The extent to which *ijtihād* continues after the Four Imams is a matter of debate. See Ibn Khaldūn, *Muqaddimat ibn Khaldūn*, 2:185-96.

[9] *Ijtihād* in the Ja'farī school (as followed by Twelver Shia Muslims) does not challenge the outlines set by Imam al-Ṣādiq or any of the other Immaculate Imams. It is distinguished from *ijtihād* in the Sunni jurisprudential schools in that it is not limited by anything outside primary religious sources. The scope of *ijtihād* is thus broader than what is found in any of the four jurisprudential schools established by Sunni Islam's Four Imams.

[10] al-Ṭabarī, *Tārīkh al-Ṭabarī*, 4:251.

all the Holy Prophet's companions. The companions were thus raised to a high level of unquestionable merit without use of the word immaculate.[11] Even when history proves infighting and bloodshed, the majority refuses to admit that one of the sides may have been wrong. To them, consideration of such conflicts should be ignored at all costs. Instead, all sides were right since all sides followed their legitimate *ijtihād*. Sunni Islam's attempt to avoid the issue of immaculacy thus resulted in their application of it in a greatly flawed way.

Theology and Jurisprudence. Integral to this debate is the disagreement over whether imamate is a theological principle or a ruling derived from juristic reasoning. What would an understanding of imamate as a ruling derived from juristic reasoning? A ruling derived from juristic reasoning is secondary. Such an understanding of imamate would basically categorize the issue as one that is subject to *ijtihād* and disagreement amongst scholars of the same school of thought. Disagreement over a juristic issue does not result in denominations and schisms.

In matters of jurisprudence, a Muslim may follow any of a set of reasoned opinions without bearing on the individual's religion, school of thought, or identity. Moreover, if imamate is to be considered a jurisprudential issue, then acting contrary to its teachings would not mean that the individual is outside the umbrella of the religion or the school of thought. On matters of theological principles (*uṣūl al-dīn*), acting in contradiction to the principle means a break with the fundamental values of the faith. To worship someone other than God would place an individual outside the banner of Islam. However, acting contrary to a jurisprudential ruling does not lead to a grave result. A person who does not pray or fast may still be a Muslim – worthy of God's chastisement, but a Muslim nonetheless.

On the other hand, a theological principle is primary and has priority. Understanding imamate as a theological principle means that it is

---

[11] It may be said that the idea of 'probity and justice of all companions' refers only to their trustworthiness and reliability. However, this does not appear to be the understanding for the majority of those who hold this view. If 'justice' meant only trustworthiness, then evidence to the contrary should be assessed and considered. However, most who ascribe to this position reject consideration of such evidence. To them, the merits of the companions are unquestionable. Regardless of the merits of such an argument, it is an ascription of immaculacy to the companions – albeit with different terminology. That said, there were some who did not shy away from using the word immaculacy. See Fakhr al-Dīn al-Rāzī, *Mafātīḥ al-ghayb (al-Tafsir al-kabir)*, exegesis of verse 4:59.

directly relevant to an individual's faith and identity. It is an issue of belief and non-belief, a defining aspect of a religion, denomination, or school of thought.[12] It is a concept that is in tandem with tawḥīd and nubuwwah.

The followers of the Holy Household have always held that imamate is an issue of theological principle. It is a matter that defines our identity as Shia Muslims. A rejection of its most fundamental values would mean that the individual has strayed outside the school of thought.

Oppression and Legitimacy. A debate between two parties can take multiple forms. Sometimes, the two parties are equal in terms of power and resources. In such a situation, each of the two parties can be forthright with its views without fear of persecution. That was not the case for Shia Muslims historically. Throughout history, the followers of the Holy Household were an oppressed minority whose views were opposed by ruling powers – with minor exceptions. This began with the growing influence of the Umayyad clan during the first century after the Hijra of the Prophet. It continued through the ages and we may still see similar forms of persecution in the current age. Many Shia were expelled from their country – their crime was that they were Shia and thus assumed to pose a threat to national security. Many also met their end in group executions and mass graves. Many have fallen victim to cycles of sectarian violence, indiscriminate bombings, and terrorism. All this persecution had a clear goal in mind – to expel the Shia from the fold of Islam. From the oppressive dynasties of the first century after Hijra, to the current sectarian extremists, the fundamental excuse for oppressing the Shia has been claims of their apostacy and heresy. But, the fundamental motivation was political. The Shia profess that the Household of the Prophet, the descendants of ʿAlī, held the highest legitimacy, while the Umayyads and the ʿAbbasids held none. Such ideas could not be tolerated in the least, as they threatened these dynasties at the core. Despite all of this, the followers of the Holy Household were able to keep a foothold within Islam and impose their presence and legitimacy despite

[12] In this sense, the differing understandings of imamate can be likened to national values and national laws. National laws are human legislated jurisprudential rulings. A person who breaks the law will face the appropriate fine or punishment. Only rarely will breaking the law result in a loss of citizenship or national identity. However, disagreement over the nation's values can lead an individual to be (or be labeled) unpatriotic. It is easier for an individual to lose citizenship by renouncing it or seeking another than by committing a felony. Civil wars begin not by mere criminal acts, but over fundamental characteristics of national identity.

those claims. We were not only able to survive, but to strengthen our core, expand our base, and become a recognized school within the body of Islam. Narrations tell us that at the time of the passing of the Holy Prophet, Imam ʿAlī only had a handful of supporters he could count on. Today, the followers of Imam ʿAlī make up a significant portion of the Muslim world. How were the Shia able to survive and thrive despite the incessant persecution? This was the result of the teachings of our Immaculate Imams. They taught us that while we cannot control others' actions, we can control our own. We may continue to face oppression and persecution, but we must never allow it to be justified. That comes with the sincere upholding of religious truths and morals. By being upstanding citizens and integral members of our societies, we begin to draw attention to our cause and disgust towards our persecutors.

Al-Naṣṣ. There is a disagreement over the necessity, existence, and meaning of designation (naṣṣ) in relation to the issue of imamate. The followers of the Holy Household always held that naṣṣ is the primary method by which we can understand imamate and know the imam. So much so, that adherence to the naṣṣ has become one of the Shia's primary doctrinal positions. Other schools of thought do not have that emphasis on naṣṣ. Some claim that it is unnecessary. Others debate whether or not it exists and dispute the meaning of any existing texts. The result was that they began to create multiple and contradicting theories about the source of legitimacy. Effectively, legitimacy became a derivative of authority, not a prerequisite to it. You find that they attempt to rationalize the political ascension of any ruler, whether it was by force, appointment, birthright, or any other manner. Thus, their theories on the subject became muddled and contradictory.[13] The result is a complete devaluation of the role of the ummah.[14] No matter who the ruler is or how he grasped the throne, his reign would be justified. No matter what atrocities are committed and what policies are instituted, the ruling power is seen as legitimate. Within such a framework, there is no role or value for the ummah in determining its destiny.

---

[13] This subject is deserving of a more extended analysis over. We have merely provided the reader with our summary position here.

[14] The whole community of Muslims bound together by ties of religion. (*Oxford Dictionary*, s.v. "umma"). Ummah is derived from the Arabic root verb *A-M-M (alif-mīm-mīm)* (to intend, seek, or aim). An ummah is literally a group sharing one aim, but generally connotes the entirety of all Muslim communities.

On the other hand, the Shia worldview stems from the value that it gives to the ummah. Our perspective is that God appointed guardians for the faith and its adherents, and we should in turn follow those divinely appointed guardians. It is out of His grace and love for His creation that He appointed these individuals to guide and lead the flock. The ummah was given the power of choice – and the responsibility to exercise their free will – allowing it to choose whether to follow these guardians or not. To the ummah's detriment and misfortune, the choice was a rejection of God's guidance.

The Platform. There is a clear disagreement on the identity of the legitimate successor to the Holy Prophet. However, our understanding of the disagreement goes far beyond personalities. At times, we see conflict arise out of an internal struggle within a single party with a single platform. In such an instance, the issue is only that of personalities – who should rise to power and who should remain in the background. Yet in the end, both are attempting to implement the same vision and goals. That was not the case with the dispute that arose after the passing of the Holy Prophet. It was not a dispute over which personality should rise, but over the underlying vision and platform. Ultimately, the Holy Household was not given a chance to implement its vision and platform, while the other side had ample opportunity to do so. But what was the victorious side able to achieve? Justice, prosperity, and civilizational advancement have all been lost. We believe that all these losses could have been averted had the ummah made the correct choice and followed its divinely appointed guardians. A study of the movements of our Immaculate Imams, starting with the Commander of the Faithful and up to the promised al-Mahdī, would allow us to draw a clear vision and platform for the ummah. Unfortunately, the brevity of this book does not allow us to delve deeper into this issue.

Worldview. Everything that the Shia endured throughout the ages was for the sake of this comprehensive worldview. It is not about a power struggle that took place centuries ago. It is about much more than that. This allows us to understand the countless sacrifices that the imams and their followers made to safeguard their creed. It allows us to understand stances made by individuals like Imam al-Ḥusayn's companions in Karbala. It allows us to understand the words of Saʿīd ibn ʿAbdullāh al-Ḥanafī, who stood before Imam al-Ḥusayn on that day and said,

> *By God, even if I knew that I would be killed, then resurrected, then burned alive, and that would happen to me repeatedly 70 times, I would not leave you until I face my death in protection of you! How would I not do so when I surely know that it is a single death after which I will reap an honor that will never fade!*[15]

This worldview was reflected in the words of Lady Fāṭimah after the passing of her father. She stood in the mosque of the Holy Prophet and eloquently described this worldview, saying,

> فجعل الله الإيمان تطهيراً لكم من الشرك، والصلاة تنزيهاً لكم عن الكبر ... وطاعتنا نظاماً للملّة، وإمامتنا أماناً من الفرقة ...

> *And thus God had made faith for you so that you may be purified from disbelief, prayer for your transcendence [away from] arrogance... and obedience to us as a framework for correct confession, and our leadership as a safeguard against disunity....*[16]

Out of all this, we can also draw some conclusions about the worldview of the school of thought of the majority. For one, their perspective is built on attempted justifications after the fact. There is no one vision or worldview that they apply consistently in their analysis of this issue. Instead, they react to what actually happened and attempt to justify the integrity of the earliest generations of those in power, as well as their current state, as being religiously legitimate – even if it is at the cost of stretching religious truths.

There was also a systemic plan to excise the Holy Household from the horizon of the majority's way of life. We find that despite unanimous acceptance of the imams' unrivalled virtue and merit, they play a minor or negligible role in the theology and religious life of the majority. You rarely find a narration or opinion from the Immaculate Imams cited in the books of the majority, even though they were the teachers of their most revered scholars.

Moreover, there were numerous attempts to distance the Shia from their imams in the minds of the majority. Any direct attack against the Holy Household was doomed to failure due to the great reverence and respect that all Muslims held toward them. The strategy thus became to

---

15 Ibn Ṭāwūs, *al-Luhūf*, 56.

16 Ibn Ṭayfūr, *Balāghat al-nisā'*, 14.

attack the Holy Household's followers, painting them as fanatics and cultists. They attempted to hide the truth that the Shia were a community established by the Holy Household; they were painted as a group of extremists with no connection to the prophet's bloodline or his spiritual heirs. Most gravely, they attempted to paint Shia Islam as a heresy and a deviance from the fold of Islam.

Our Immaculate Imams stood in the face of this latter accusation and taught us to never fall prey to its traps. They taught us to hold dearly to our identity as Muslims who adhere to the true faith as taught by the Holy Household. This allowed us to endure the oppression and persecution of political power, and even thrive in spite of it.

Readers should reflect on all these sacrifices and points, in addition to the vast heritage of teachings passed down by generations of the most trusted disciples of the Holy Household. A study of this heritage will make it clear that the Twelver Shiʿi tradition represents the school of the Holy Household and they are the true representatives of Islam.

CONCEPTUAL FRAMEWORK

Linguistic Analysis

Before we delve deeper into the topic, let us first address the linguistic roots of the concept of imamate (*imamate*).

The word comes from the root verb *A-M-M (alif-mīm-mīm)*, which means to intend, seek, or aim. The verb goes beyond passive intent, signifying an individual's active seeking of a particular aim. One derivation of this root verb is *ummah*, a group sharing a single aim. An *imam* is an individual which the *ummah* follows in pursuit of its shared aim. An imam is a leader towards a particular goal. The *ma'mūm* is the follower of the imam's actions and teachings.

This root verb and its derivatives revolve around the ideas of intent, active pursuit, objective, the pursuer, guide, leader, and motivator. We can thus see that imamate, linguistically speaking, is the advance of one individual in front of a group so that they may follow him in pursuit of an objective.

This definition is distinct from that of prophethood – the concept of a divinely appointed conveyer of God's messages, warnings, and glad tidings. An individual may hold either of these titles or may even hold both titles at the same time. The twelve Immaculate successors of the Holy Prophet Muḥammad, for example, hold the title of Imam but not prophet.

It is important to note that imamate, linguistically speaking, does not distinguish between vice and virtue. The concept reflects a group's endeavor towards a goal without evaluating the merits of that goal. Understanding the value neutrality of the term will allow us to better understand the usage of the word imam in some Qur'anic verses and noble traditions – including, for example, references to 'imams of misguidance.'

Before we continue to analyze fully the meaning of imamate, we should point out the scholastic and practical importance of beginning at the linguistic meaning. Often times, we find the linguistic understanding of technical concepts to be illuminating in their simplicity. Starting with a word's etymology allows us to establish a basic understanding of a concept before unraveling the layers of meaning that come with technical and other usages. Technical definitions often fall in line with the linguistic meaning and may add further detail and complexity.

Even when a term goes through the process of semantic change and shifts from its original linguistic meaning to a new meaning, the linguistic definition can still provide great insight. The old and new meanings are often connected in some way. For example, word usage can change from a narrower to a broader meaning, or vice versa. Scholars of etymology and semantics dedicate time to studying such phenomena. All this is to say that the linguistic understanding of a word is a useful and important starting point for a more in-depth analysis.

ON PRACTICAL AND THEORETICAL REASON

Having addressed the linguistic meaning of imamate, let us turn to the conceptual framework that underpins our understanding of the concept. We contend that the role of imamate is a natural result of the way in which God ordered both human society and the nature of our rational faculty. The Imam is an expression of the moral processes that guide one's practical reason.

The human is a manifestly complex creature. We are made of a multitude of powers and faculties that make up each one of us. Each of these faculties plays a role in the individual's makeup. Collectively, they are an individual's character. Everything that transpires in an individual goes back to the interplay of these faculties. Everything that transpires in human history is a result of the interplay of these faculties in individual human beings and in the collective of humanity.

The problem with these faculties is that they are blind. They are like machines. Each drives the individual to satisfy a particular goal without constraints. An individual's appetites, hunger and lust, seek satisfaction by any means. Ambition drives the individual to seek excellence without a true assessment of the means or verifying whether the aim is truly excellent or not. Humanity has often scorched the earth with its wrath. These faculties, in themselves, do not lead an individual towards nobility and virtue.

What does 'human rights' or 'animal rights' mean to an individual driven by the faculties of hunger, lust, and anger? What does virtue mean to an individual driven solely by ambition? These concepts are outside the realm of these faculties. Each of these faculties is like a mechanical saw – it tears through anything in its way just to continue its programmed motion. You cannot expect it to stop of its own accord out of consideration for law or morality.

This description of the human faculties applies broadly, with a single shining exception seen in human reason. Reason is the faculty that allows us to recognize, understand, and ponder on the concepts of 'harmony,' 'compromise,' 'right,' 'duty,' 'law,' or 'morality.' But before delving deeper into the faculty of reason, let us first make a few notes on the interplay of the remaining faculties.

We find that an individual who is under the influence of these faculties fails to respond effectively to each one of them. An individual cannot be completely driven by wrath, lust, sloth, pride, and all the other faculties. Each of these faculties have different, and sometimes contradictory, goals. In addition, these faculties' goals often go against social pressures that come in the form of norms and values. We may find that an individual might be driven by lust or wrath towards a particular goal, but may be dissuaded from it due to social pressures.

Moreover, these faculties often work against humanity's natural tendency of seeking excellence. When an individual sees that each of these faculties is drawing him in a certain direction, he rationally concludes that he cannot and should not attempt to satisfy them all.

At this point, it becomes evident that there needs to be a faculty that reins in these competing forces. Otherwise, humanity would be doomed to live in a state of constant internal and external strife, being driven and influenced by these contradictory forces. Without a superior faculty to regulate and organize these faculties, this strife would be meaningless and unending. This superior faculty can control and even suppress the rest of the faculties in service of its goal. It allows the individual to find balance in life and silence the incessant demands of each of the faculties. It allows the individual to recognize and abide by concepts such as 'law' and 'morality.'

This superior faculty can even convert these passions into positive forces for the progress of humanity. It can go beyond simple suppression of their incessant and mechanical influences, and use them as tools within a higher legal, ethical, or philosophical framework.

This superior faculty is what philosophers have referred to as *practical reason* (*al-ʿaql al-ʿamalī*). Practical reason's constant deliberation, judgement, and decision making permits the individual to regulate and control all the other faculties. It allows each one of us to direct our passions and internal forces towards a purpose that we define.

Practical reason is closely related to *theoretical reason* (*al-ʿaql al-naẓarī*) – the faculty of conceptualization, understanding, and problem solving that makes metaphysical sense of ourselves and our cosmos. Theoretical reason is the faculty that perceives and conceives laws, morals, and goals, while practical reason is the aspect of our intellect that applies those rational conclusions. In this respect, theoretical reason comprises the legislative functions of our intellect, while practical reason comprises the executive functions.

THE ROLES OF PRACTICAL REASON

Practical reason plays three important roles in its mastery over the remainder of the faculties.[1]

First, practical reason regulates each and every faculty to ensure that it remains within its moral boundaries. It communicates with each of the faculties and ensures that it is satisfied, but only to the proper extent and through the proper means. It ensures that hunger does not lead to gluttony and that sexual desire does not lead to promiscuity.

Second, practical reason ensures a balance between these faculties, especially when they become at odds with one another. What happens if an individual's ambition pulls in one direction while shyness tugs in the

[1] Practical reason functions as both a perceptive and executive faculty. As a perceptive faculty, it perceives moral propositions related to action such as what one 'ought to do' and 'ought not to do.' In its perceptive function, practical reason overlaps with theoretical reason. In its executive function, practical reason acts on these propositions that it perceives. Both the perceptive and executive functions of practical reason are in play during the exercise of its three roles.

other? What happens when a person's vanity tells them to spend, but their frugality says otherwise? In these situations, practical reason steps in to balance these opposing forces. Practical reason draws upon the process of the theoretical reason in order to create balance between the faculties.

A look at Aristotelian ethics helps us better understand these two roles. Aristotle said that each sphere of action or feeling – what we have been calling the faculties – can be exercised either in excess, deficiency, or balance. Excess or deficiency in a faculty are vices, while balance is virtue.[2] For example, an individual may have an excess of confidence that will lead them to be rash and foolhardy. A deficiency in confidence will make an individual weak and cowardly. Virtue is in having the right balance of confidence, which translates into courage.

The job of practical reason is to find this balance for each of the faculties, as well as lead the individual towards virtue by balancing the whole of the faculties.

Third, practical reason seeks to achieve a balance between the individual and society. We see in cultures and philosophies across the world that there are different emphases placed on the individual versus the community. Some philosophies and cultures see communality as the supreme good with the individual always expected to sacrifice for the greater good. Other philosophies and cultures see the individual and its liberty as the center of their ethics, with the community's role being to serve each individual within it.[3] Practical reason seeks a balance between these two views, such that the individual and the community share a bond of mutual benefit.

Having understood these roles of practical reason, it is important to direct readers' attention to one important caveat. Practical reason's role as a balancing and guiding force does not mean that it is always in control. Individuals often act irrationally, especially in pursuit of desire and satisfaction of the base faculties such as hunger and lust. Practical reason's guidance may be ignored and sidelined, overcome by the other faculties. While virtue lies in applying practical reason, not all men are

---

[2] This is Aristotle's concept of virtue and the doctrine of the mean found in *Nicomachean Ethics* II.5–6, 1105b–1107a.

[3] In ethics, this is known as the conflict between communitarianism and liberalism. See: Bell, 'Communitarianism', *The Stanford Encyclopedia of Philosophy*. See also: Gaus, Courtland, and Schmidtz, 'Liberalism', *The Stanford Encyclopedia of Philosophy*.

virtuous. While practical reason may be more sublime than the other faculties, it remains a force amongst others, and may overcome or be overcome by the others.

Society as Macrocosm

Having understood the operation of these faculties within the human individual, let us turn our attention to their operation on a macro level. Philosophers, Muslim and otherwise, have often seen society as a macrocosm of the human individual. If this understanding is true, we should be able to see the same operations we discussed above working on a grander scale.

It is not our purpose here to establish that the world operates in this particular way. This discussion is meant to be illustrative and insightful with proper academic rigor left to deeper philosophical studies. Some philosophers have dedicated time and effort to the study of these concepts, and their work should be given its due right. For the purposes of this book, we draw the attention of the reader towards the concept merely to illustrate its value.

Indeed, we can see these forces and faculties operate in a very similar way when we analyze human society in general. We find that each individual may during their lives manifest one or more of these forces. This may be seen in individual actions influenced by the particular faculty, or even consistently throughout the individual's lifetime. When an individual acts in accordance to their own greed, they leave that mark on the world around them. When an individual is consistently influenced and controlled by their greed, they become a manifestation of it in society. Individuals of this nature collectively represent the force of greed within humanity. They interact and compete with the forces of wrath, lust, pride, and all the other faculties embedded in human nature. If greed takes hold of a nation, it will begin to prioritize monetary gain and materialistic prosperity over labor conditions, environmental quality, and other moral concerns. If wrath takes hold, the nation will become militaristic and descend into war at the smallest provocation.

We can easily see how many of the world's global problems can be rooted in the influence and competition of these forces. Wrath can lead to global warfare that drains humanity's energies in futile bloodshed. Greed can lead us to make decisions that have a catastrophic effect on

Earth's environment. Pride and envy may lead a group to the ethnic cleansing of another.

Here, reason plays an important role in balancing and directing these forces.

Just as reason plays a role within the internal makeup of human individuals, it also plays a role in the makeup of human society. Reason applied on a societal scale provides the necessary balance between the forces and faculties that draw humanity towards disaster. Reason allows us to identify the individual good and the societal good and find a balance between the two. It allows us to understand social and environmental responsibility. It allows us to establish the rule of law under the protection of due process. If exercised properly, reason allows for the control of the destructive faculties of greed, anger, and the rest.

And just as an individual's intellect can be understood as theoretical and practical, the same can be applied on a societal scale. In other words, society is in need of external theoretical and practical reason, alongside the internal theoretical and practical reason that each individual possesses.

Internal theoretical reason provides each individual with axiomatic principles, syllogistic forms of reasoning, and other tools through which they can drive towards excellence. Yet an individual's internal theoretical reason is not enough to reach the greatest levels of excellence. From a young age, our parents begin to teach us everything from language to sports to morality. We grow and become reliant on teachers through grade school, then on instructors and professors at colleges and universities. Our parents, teachers, instructors, and professors all play a role as part of society's external theoretical reason – shaping the way each of us thinks and behaves.

Beyond the level of our individual need for this external source, we find that human societies are heavily reliant – if not entirely dependent – on experts and public intellectuals. We rely on experts to ensure that air traffic is properly controlled and that drugs are properly tested and approved. Moreover, each society takes pride in the great thinkers – its geniuses – that emerge to give their nations an intellectual stimulus. Societies take pride in generating the likes of Socrates, Hume, and Einstein, to name a few.

The pinnacle of humanity's external theoretical reason is embodied in God's appointed prophets. Their role is to effect excellence in human reason in every way.[4] They do not in any way limit or dispossess humanity of their free rational thought. Following them does not make us primitive. Rather, each of them is like a prestigious university. Their mission is to develop the rational capacity of their students so that they can rise to the highest levels of excellence.

That is why we find human society making leaps in their development when they follow the leadership of their prophets. Take the biblical example of Moses who led the Israelites from being a disadvantaged and enslaved people in Egypt to becoming a regional power under the leadership of David and Solomon. Or the example of the Prophet Muḥammad, whose teachings allowed tribal Arab societies to advance from their nomadic roots to become a diverse, global civilization, greatly contributing to the arts and sciences during the height of the ʿAbbasid Empire. Their successes were due to following the teachings of their prophets, while their failures – moral and material – were due to abandoning their teachings. Had each society followed the teachings of its prophets and chosen divine leaders more closely, the path of human advancement would have been much simpler and more expedient.

In the same way, the pinnacle of humanity's external practical reason is imamate. The role of the imam is to be the greatest leader, the best manager, and the finest educator. It is humanity's misfortune and the fruits of its poor decision making that these individuals were not allowed to exercise their role to its fullest extent. Of course, imams are not meant to limit our decision making or dispossess us of our free will. As is the case with prophets, an imam's role is to aid humanity in its advancement towards excellence. Their role is to set the highest example through their leadership and conduct. The best example of that can be seen in the short years that Imam ʿAlī ibn Abī Ṭālib ruled the Muslim ummah as its caliph – and the long years in which he did not. The examples of immaculate leadership, with all its tolerance, are too many to recount here.

Prophethood and imamate are not just theoretical constructs. They hold great practical significance. Imamate is not just a historical issue revolving around who should have held political authority during some point in history. It is about much more than that. It is about achieving that vision of having practical reason in its absolute and immaculate form, leading us to develop and advance our future – away from the push and

---

[4] See: al-Ḥillī, *Kashf al-murād*, 468–70.

pull of anger, greed, and the other faculties that have led to countless tragedies in human history. Imamate is about the divine promise that the oppressed shall inherit the Earth:

وَنُرِيدُ أَن نَّمُنَّ عَلَى الَّذِينَ اسْتُضْعِفُوا فِي الْأَرْضِ وَنَجْعَلَهُمْ أَئِمَّةً وَنَجْعَلَهُمُ الْوَارِثِينَ

And We desire to show favor to those who were abased in the land, and to make them imams, and to make them the heirs.[5]

[5] The Holy Qur'an, 28:5.

CONCEPTUAL COROLLARIES

From the preceding conceptual understanding of imamate, we can begin to formulate a number of corollaries that allow us to understand the concept in more detail. The following eight corollaries are drawn from the explanation we have outlined above with the addition of some inferences drawn from the Holy Qur'an and noble traditions. We do not seek to provide definitive proofs for each of these conclusions. Instead, we present them as our explanation of imamate. The purpose is to clarify how we perceive and understand the concept, both for clarity's sake and for the sake of providing a frame of reference for coming discussions.

Imamate Starts with the Self

The imam is the individual in whom reason exerts absolute control over all other faculties. Practical reason in such an individual does not stop at his own faculties. It extends to exert influence over others around him.

There are individuals in this world who have reached a completely opposite position. They allowed their base faculties to subvert their reason. To them, reasoning became a tool to advance their greed and wrath. Such individuals also exert an influence over others around them, leading them towards that same path. Such individuals are the imams of misguidance that are referenced in the Holy Qur'an and the noble traditions.

Leadership is something that starts with the self. We cannot imagine an individual who walks the path of misguidance but can lead others towards the path of reason. Neither can we imagine an individual who has perfected the control of practical reason over the base faculties, but who purposely acts to misguide others. God says in the Holy Qur'an,

وَإِذِ ابْتَلَىٰ إِبْرَاهِيمَ رَبُّهُ بِكَلِمَاتٍ فَأَتَمَّهُنَّ ۖ قَالَ إِنِّي جَاعِلُكَ لِلنَّاسِ إِمَامًا ۖ قَالَ وَمِن ذُرِّيَّتِي ۖ قَالَ
لَا يَنَالُ عَهْدِي الظَّالِمِينَ

> *When his Lord tested Abraham with certain words and he fulfilled them, He said, 'I am making you the Imam of mankind.' Said he, 'And from among my descendants?' He said, 'My pledge does not extend to the unjust.'*[1]

The unjust are not capable of undertaking the role of the imam. It is not just a punishment for their injustices, but a natural outcome of their evil actions. An individual cannot become an imam, leading others to perfect their practical reason if he does not hold that perfection in himself. The unjust – individuals whose practical reason lost the battle against the base passions – are not qualified or capable of becoming imams. An imam cannot be just a mouthpiece. An imam must set the example.

Immaculacy of the Imam

Having understood imamate as the personification of reason, we can conclude that the imam must be immaculate. Error in thought, actions, and behavior come as a result of the base passions taking control of the individual. However, an individual who acts solely in accordance to reason will not err.[2] Theoretical reason ensures that he properly understands the implications of his actions, while practical reason ensures that he follows through with the appropriate decision. As such, it is said that the angels – beings which embody reason without desire – are infallible.[3] As for those individuals who have been granted the full range

---

[1] The Holy Qur'an, 2:124.

[2] An individual who unfailingly follows the dictates of reason will not commit any intentional error. But what about unintentional errors? That requires a special form of divine grace in addition to the aforementioned blessing from God. This grace is bestowed upon the individual in order to uphold the function and status of guarding the message in word and in action, without any error. This allows the imam to maintain the absolute confidence of reasonable people regarding the integrity of his guardianship.

[3] An individual or thing which is *infallible* is "incapable of error" - *Merriam-Webster Dictionary*. In this text, we distinguish between infallibility and immaculacy. While both may be called *'iṣmah* in Arabic, infallibility connotes an inability to err. However, our understanding of *'iṣmah* in our prophets, messengers, and imams is that they are capable of error but are safeguarded from it by their own choice and by divine grace.

of human faculties but were able to ensure reason's absolute control over them, they are the ones whom we refer to as immaculate.[4]

THE IMAMS OF MISGUIDANCE

From the foregoing, we can also draw a conclusion about the imams of misguidance. They stand in complete opposition to the imams of guidance whom we described above. The two are like light and darkness, or like reason and ignorance. The imams of misguidance are individuals who have allowed their base desires to exert complete control, allowing their reason to become a subservient tool to the powers of their base desires.

From this we understand the statement of the Holy Prophet when he said during the battle of Aḥzāb,

برز الايمان كله إلى الكفر كله

Surely, absolute faith has set out against absolute disbelief.[5]

He described Imam ʿAlī as absolute faith because he embodied absolute reason. On the other side stood a force that wanted to eradicate the light of reason. A force such as that cannot be called anything but absolute disbelief.

IMAMATE AND GUIDANCE

The next philosophical conclusion drawn from our previous discussions can be used to answer a number of prevalent misconceptions about religion. That is, that imamate - and religion more generally - is about providing holistic guidance to humanity in every level of our development.

To better understand this point, let us first summarize some of the critiques posed against religion:

Religion is an oppressive sociopolitical construct. There are some who would portray religion as a socio-political construct founded for the purpose of controlling and subjugating the masses. Such individuals

---

[4] *Immaculacy* is the state of having or containing no flaw or error - *Merriam-Webster Dictionary*. In this text, we use the word immaculacy as a translation of the Arabic *ʿiṣmah* specifically when it relates to prophets, messengers, and imams. The word *ʿiṣmah* is a derivation of the root *ʿ-Ṣ-M (ʿayn - ṣād – mīm)* which means 'impede or protect.' In Shia theology, a person who is *maʿṣūm* (immaculate) is one who is safeguarded - by their own choice and by divine grace - from any flaw or error.

[5] al-Majlisī, *Biḥār al-anwār*, 39:1.

look at how religion was used by authoritarian figures throughout history as a tool to legitimize their conduct. There are countless examples that can be given in this regard. It can be seen in the most primitive societies and their use of patron deities to mobilize the masses for war. It can be seen in East Asia when an emperor declares himself the Son of Heaven with a divine mandate to govern, or in Western Europe when a king declares his reign to be in accord with the will of divine providence. We do not wish to dispute the fact that religion was misused by individuals who held political authority. Muslim history is full of examples of such misuse. The most prominent example may be that of Yazīd's justifications for the massacre of Karbala. However, we take issue with the fallacy of equating the misuse of religion with the claim that it was founded for the sake of subjugation.

Religion suppresses scientific progress. Another popular misconception is that religion is in conflict with scientific progress. The most prominent example cited by proponents of this view is the trial and condemnation of Galileo by the Church for his views on astronomy. Holy scriptures contain some explanations of natural phenomena that seem to conflict with scientific theories and explanations. The claim is that the religious community's attachment to holy scripture distances them from science and objective rational analysis. This view – more popular amongst laymen than in the scientific community – sets aside the long and varied history of religious individuals leading at the forefront of scientific discoveries as they attempt to understand the works of the Creator. It conflates religion with the views of a few extremists in the religious community who continue to advocate theories such as that of a flat Earth without any real basis in religious knowledge.

Religion is a set of primitive dogmas and rituals. Yet another attack characterizes people of religion as primitive, incapable of progressing along with the rest of the world. They think of religion as a set of rituals created by human primitive imagination for one reason or another. They see religious teachings as nothing more than an archaic tool that no longer serves a purpose in this day and age.

These three points can be summarized in one accusation – that religion restricts and obstructs human reason and progress. As we will see, this accusation has no grounding in reality. We do not wish to provide detailed counter arguments to these points in this book. We do not wish to demonstrate the reality of God's existence and the truth of our religion.

These can be found in the many works of our scholars written specifically on these topics. For the purpose of this treatise, we wish to demonstrate how our understanding of religion in general, and imamate in particular, renders arguments such as these incongruous.

Let us reflect further on the relationship between religion and reason. Even a cursory view of our religion demonstrates the great value that it places on the exercise of reason. Numerous verses of the Holy Qur'an and a large body of noble traditions urge us to develop our intellect and be rational in every aspect of our lives. God Almighty says in the Holy Book,

كِتَابٌ أَنزَلْنَاهُ إِلَيْكَ مُبَارَكٌ لِّيَدَّبَّرُوا آيَاتِهِ وَلِيَتَذَكَّرَ أُولُو الْأَلْبَابِ

> *[This is] a blessed Book that We have sent down to you, so that they may contemplate its signs, and that those who possess intellect may take admonition.*[6]

The Holy Prophet and our Immaculate Imams also emphasized the importance of exercising reason. Imam Ṣādiq said,

حديث تدريه خير من الف حديث ترويه

> *One tradition that you understand is better than a thousand that you narrate [but do not understand].*[7]

If we look at the religious sciences, we find that they are rooted in methodical rational processes. At the very beginning of their scholastic journey, a student of the seminary must study logic as a basis for all other studies. The sciences of philosophy and theology are built on rational proof. The principles of jurisprudence are derived from logical and epistemological origins. Our faith's emphasis on reason is not only theoretical but is consistently applied by our scholars at every level of their work.

The reader should realize that the critiques of religion come in many different forms and at many levels. They may even come from faithful believers who, for one reason or another, fall victim to a twisted version of these fallacies. Some would undermine the idea of imamate and say, 'We are not incompetent to be in need of guardians holding authority over us.' Others seek to escape the shackles of religious expertise and claim that they can understand the faith through their own readings of

---

[6] The Holy Qur'an, 38:29.

[7] al-Ṣadūq, *Ma'ānī al-bkhbār*, 2.

religious texts. They try to impose their preferred interpretation of a 'progressive' religion away from cumbersome obligations prescribed by expert research.

It is important to note that no system, philosophy, or movement can escape the idea of obligation. We may think of a democratic state as an ideal of liberty. However, in reality citizens willingly give up some of their liberty to become obligated by the actions of their elected governors. Every day, we willingly give up a degree of freedom when we blindly follow the expertise of physicians and engineers. A nation's physicians are allowed to become the trustees of public health. Politicians are given the role as trustees over domestic and foreign policies. Why, then, do we decry the trusteeship of religious experts over the believers when it comes to intricate matters of the faith?

LEADERSHIP AND POLITICS

Within our theology, imamate holds an important existential role as the external manifestation of the collective practical reason of humans. Imamate is often characterized as merely a legislative issue – God appointed an imam and commanded us to follow. And while divine command bears a heavy weight, our understanding of the existential value of imamate gives it even greater meaning. An imam is not an imam because he is followed. An imam is an imam by divine providence, command and decree. In other words, what gives divine leadership its value is what God bestowed upon it at creation, and not whether or not people follow this leadership. That is why our scholars say that imamate is an office that cannot possibly be usurped, even if historically the legitimate imam is not allowed the freedom to exercise the functions of his office.

To draw an example, think of a physicist. She might be hired as part of a product development team in a small company. She might be hired by NASA and contribute to some grand discovery about the universe. She might become a professor at a university and become an educator by profession. Or she may not be hired in the first place and sit at home unemployed. None of these scenarios would make her any more or any less of a physicist; they do not diminish her qualifications.

The point is to distinguish between characteristics that individuals hold out of merit, and the roles and responsibilities that may relate to these characteristics but do not affect the individuals' merit.

The problem is that when we think of imamate, we allow ourselves to get bogged down by the socio-political history. We submit ourselves to others' narrative. We begin to think of it as a struggle over political supremacy.

What if someone were to say, 'Political authority is a definitive part of holistic leadership'? Even if we assume that the underlying premise is true, the correct way to frame the historical intellectual debate is not over 'who should have governed.' Rather, it is a debate over defining the proper qualifications for leadership. Imamate is not about the legal and political rights of the imam. It is about their existential merit and their proper role in guidance.

This is why historically, the Immaculate Imams from the household of the Holy Prophet did not stop all activity when they were denied their correct place as the legitimate authority over the Muslim ummah. They continued to advance their project of guidance from outside the halls of political power. Their movement did not focus on establishing an empire under their rule, but on creating a group of followers who understood their teachings. The fact that they did not hold political power meant that their project was met with many impediments and delays, but they continued regardless. It is simply the Muslim ummah's misfortune and the ill outcome of its choices that led us towards this path.

Imamate and Knowledge

Imamate is a position of merit earned through an individual's attainment of knowledge – not any knowledge but a specific form that allows the individual to reach the high status of imamate. This knowledge is not given arbitrarily to certain individuals. Rather, it is earned through a process of trials, patience, and certitude that allow the individual to gain the secrets of the unseen. We will speak more about this knowledge and how it is attained later in this treatise, especially when we tackle the Qur'anic view of imamate.

It is this knowledge that leads to the imam's merit and position, which leads to our great love and devotion for these individuals. Our worldview is based on this natural existential merit, and not based on the human constructs of leadership and political authority.

We should also mention a technical term that readers may come across in further readings. Our scholars say that this knowledge gives rise to what we call the power of *malakūt* (dominion) or *al-walāyah al-*

takwīniyyah in the imam. This power allows its holder to exercise guardianship over its subject. As such, the imam becomes part of the causal system of this subject. Our scholars have differing views over what this means exactly, and an exposé of these opinions is beyond the scope of this work.

Perfecting Reason

The excellence of theoretical reason comes through practical reason. Theoretical reason cannot fulfil its full potential unless it is applied. Nor is it meaningful if it is impossible to apply. Practical reason completes the theoretical by taking it outside the mind, beyond the hypothetical, and applying it to reality.

We can see this premise throughout the history of science. At many junctures, polymaths would use their knowledge of math and science to come up with marvelous inventions. Sometimes, they were simply wrong about the physics of their inventions, making their work inapplicable and useless. At other times, these inventors had the right ideas but did not have the necessary materials – like coal or aluminum – to allow their knowledge to become a technological reality. Their ideas were brought to excellence by successive applications of practical reason.

Take the example of the car. Practical reason allows us to take it outside the realm of algebra, geometry, and physics, and into reality. Moreover, practical reason allowed for the use of interchangeable parts and the assembly line to create a mass-market vehicle. At the same time, none of that would have been possible without the theoretical understanding of math and physics.

When the Muslims spurned the Holy Prophet's household, they claimed to attach themselves to the theoretical reason embodied by the Holy Qur᾿an and prophetic teachings. Yet by marginalizing the imams, they rejected the practical reason that exemplifies and completes the theoretical. That is why Imam 'Alī said in the early days after the passing of the Holy Prophet,

احْتَجُّوا بِالشَّجَرَةِ، وَأَضَاعُوا الثَّمَرَةَ.

> *They have presented the tree as evidence, but neglected the fruit.*[8]

---

[8] al-Raḍī, *Nahj al-balāghah*, Sermon 67.

IMPORTANCE OF IMAMATE

Knowing that the role of the imam as humanity's external practical reason is similar to the role of practical reason in the individual, we can draw some conclusions about the role and importance of the imam's being. For example, just as it is the role of practical reason to find a balance between individual and social benefits, it is the imam's role to find that same balance. This is not a simple task. To take away from one and give the other, without committing injustice to either, is a delicate balance that is rarely achieved. It is this kind of intricate role that the imam is meant to fulfill.

As we discussed before, if the individual's faculties are left unchecked by practical reason, they will come to control and lead to the individual's demise. The same is true of society as a whole. If the powers of greed and wrath are allowed to control without the check of reason, society will be doomed. Just as the lack of practical reason would lead to the demise of an individual, the lack of an external practical reason would lead to the demise of humanity. From this we can understand narrations such as the one by Imam al-Bāqir who said,

لو أن الامام رفع من الأرض ساعة لماجت بأهلها

> *If the imam were to be removed from the Earth for an hour, it would be cast into chaos with its people.*

We read in *al-Ziyārah al-jāmiʿah al-kabīrah* – the Grand Comprehensive Visitation of our beloved imams – the following,

ذِكْرُكُمْ فِي الذَّاكِرِينَ وَأَسْمَاؤُكُمْ فِي الْأَسْمَاءِ وَأَجْسَادُكُمْ فِي الْأَجْسَادِ وَأَرْوَاحُكُمْ فِي الْأَرْوَاحِ
وَأَنْفُسُكُمْ فِي النُّفُوسِ وَآثَارُكُمْ فِي الْآثَارِ وَقُبُورُكُمْ فِي الْقُبُورِ فَمَا أَحْلَى أَسْمَاءَكُمْ وَأَكْرَمَ أَنْفُسَكُمْ
وَأَعْظَمَ شَأْنَكُمْ وَأَجَلَّ خَطَرَكُمْ وَأَوْفَى عَهْدَكُمْ وَأَصْدَقَ وَعْدَكُمْ

> *Your remembrance is amongst those who remember! Your names are amongst names! Your figures are amongst figures! Your souls are amongst souls! Your selves are amongst selves! Your traditions are amongst traditions! Your graves are amongst graves!*
>
> *How sweet are your names! How noble are your selves! How grand is your position! How magnificent is your station! How trustworthy is your covenant! How true is your promise!*

What do these words mean? What do we mean when we tell our imam that 'his name is amongst names'? A precise understanding of this passage shows us both the similarity and distinction between the imam and the followers. Their names are like other names, but are the sweetest of names! Their figures are like other figures, but are the most towering of figures! Their souls are like other souls, but are the purest of souls! Their selves are like other selves, but have a divinely endowed charisma that gives them command over others, leading them towards the path of guidance!

The theoretical understanding of imamate that we have outlined so far allows us to better understand the status of our imams as laid out in the supplications and visitations that they taught us.

QUR'ANIC FRAMEWORK

Having laid out a conceptual framework for imamate, let us turn to briefly outline a Qur'anic framework for the concept. As we will see, the Holy Qur'an is replete with verses that address the concept. Let us read through these verses and glean out an understanding that will aid us in the coming discussions.

Qur'anic Imamate

There are three groups of Qur'anic verses that we wish to address here.

First, God says in the Holy Qur'an,

إِنَّمَا أَنتَ مُنذِرٌ ۖ وَلِكُلِّ قَوْمٍ هَادٍ

You are only a warner, and there is a guide for every people.[1]

This verse signifies the continuous nature of imamate.

Second, let us look at the verses revealed on the Day of Ghadīr Khumm. God says,

يَا أَيُّهَا الرَّسُولُ بَلِّغْ مَا أُنزِلَ إِلَيْكَ مِن رَّبِّكَ ۖ وَإِن لَّمْ تَفْعَلْ فَمَا بَلَّغْتَ رِسَالَتَهُ

O Apostle! Communicate that which has been sent down to you from your Lord, and if you do not, you will not have communicated His message.[2]

---

1 The Holy Qur'an, 13:7.

2 The Holy Qur'an, 5:67.

This verse signifies the importance of imamate within the framework of the completion of the prophetic mission. The Holy Prophet was not given such a command in regards to any other matter of the faith. Imamate is equated to prophethood here with the entire message being declared meaningless if this integral part was not delivered. God also says,

الْيَوْمَ يَئِسَ الَّذِينَ كَفَرُوا مِن دِينِكُمْ فَلَا تَخْشَوْهُمْ وَاخْشَوْنِ

Today the faithless have despaired of your religion. So do not fear them, but fear Me.[3]

God declares to the believers that they should no longer fear any external force that tries to destroy their religion. With imamate, God has protected the faith from all its faithless external enemies. The verse continues,

الْيَوْمَ أَكْمَلْتُ لَكُمْ دِينَكُمْ وَأَتْمَمْتُ عَلَيْكُمْ نِعْمَتِي وَرَضِيتُ لَكُمُ الْإِسْلَامَ دِينًا

Today I have perfected your religion for you, and I have completed My blessing upon you, and I have approved Islam as your religion.[4]

Again, these verses highlight the importance of imamate as an integral part of the faith. It was on the Day of Ghadīr Khumm that God perfected the religion and completed His blessings. The Holy Prophet had spent twenty-three years preaching the message of God. He delivered the essential teachings from prayer to pilgrimage and from monotheism to divine judgement. But it was with the event of Ghadīr that God Almighty declared that the religion of Islam had been completed and perfected.

In another verse God says,

إِنَّ عَلَيْنَا لَلْهُدَىٰ

Indeed, it is [incumbent] upon Us to guide.[5]

This verse signifies that the issue of imamate is one mandated by God. God has prescribed mercy upon Himself, and guidance is a form of mercy. It is He who provides guidance and appoints guides for humanity. We have no say in this, as we have no say in the issue of prophethood. God Almighty says,

وَمَا كَانَ لِمُؤْمِنٍ وَلَا مُؤْمِنَةٍ إِذَا قَضَى اللَّهُ وَرَسُولُهُ أَمْرًا أَن يَكُونَ لَهُمُ الْخِيَرَةُ مِنْ أَمْرِهِمْ

---

[3] The Holy Qur'an, 5:3.

[4] The Holy Qur'an, 5:3.

[5] The Holy Qur'an, 92:12.

And it is not for a believing man or a believing woman, when God and His Messenger have decreed a matter, to have a choice regarding the matter.[6]

The Holy Qur'an also relays a pertinent conversation between God and Prophet Abraham.

وَإِذِ ابْتَلَىٰ إِبْرَاهِيمَ رَبُّهُ بِكَلِمَاتٍ فَأَتَمَّهُنَّ ۖ قَالَ إِنِّي جَاعِلُكَ لِلنَّاسِ إِمَامًا ۖ قَالَ وَمِن ذُرِّيَّتِي ۖ قَالَ لَا يَنَالُ عَهْدِي الظَّالِمِينَ

When his Lord tested Abraham with certain words and he fulfilled them, He said, 'I am making you the Imam of mankind.' He said, 'And from among my descendants?' He said, 'My pledge does not extend to the unjust.'[7]

We can draw several conclusions from this verse. We can see that imamate is not only distinct from prophethood, but is of an even greater status. Abraham was a prophet of God who carried His message. Yet even as a prophet, he had to be tested before he was given the spiritual station of imam. And when Abraham asked that this status be conferred to his descendants, God told him that the prerequisite for holding this high position must be met. It will not be granted to the unjust who are not fit to hold this lofty status. Still, God answered Abraham's prayer and chose from among the just of his descendants to hold this status. God says in His Holy Book,

إِنَّ اللَّهَ اصْطَفَىٰ آدَمَ وَنُوحًا وَآلَ إِبْرَاهِيمَ وَآلَ عِمْرَانَ عَلَى الْعَالَمِينَ

Indeed Allah chose Adam and Noah, and the progeny of Abraham and the progeny of Imran above all the nations.[8]

The story of Abraham gives us great insight into the prerequisites of imamate. The Holy Qur'an relays the story as follows,

فَبَشَّرْنَاهُ بِغُلَامٍ حَلِيمٍ ۞ فَلَمَّا بَلَغَ مَعَهُ السَّعْيَ قَالَ يَا بُنَيَّ إِنِّي أَرَىٰ فِي الْمَنَامِ أَنِّي أَذْبَحُكَ فَانظُرْ مَاذَا تَرَىٰ ۚ قَالَ يَا أَبَتِ افْعَلْ مَا تُؤْمَرُ ۖ سَتَجِدُنِي إِن شَاءَ اللَّهُ مِنَ الصَّابِرِينَ ۞ فَلَمَّا أَسْلَمَا وَتَلَّهُ لِلْجَبِينِ ۞ وَنَادَيْنَاهُ أَن يَا إِبْرَاهِيمُ ۞ قَدْ صَدَّقْتَ الرُّؤْيَا ۚ إِنَّا كَذَٰلِكَ نَجْزِي الْمُحْسِنِينَ ۞ إِنَّ هَٰذَا لَهُوَ الْبَلَاءُ الْمُبِينُ

So We gave him the good news of a forbearing son. When he was old enough to assist in his endeavor, he said, 'My son! I see in

---

[6] The Holy Qur'an, 33:36.

[7] The Holy Qur'an, 2:124.

[8] The Holy Qur'an, 3:33.

dreams that I am sacrificing you. See what you think.' He said, 'Father! Do whatever you have been commanded. If Allah wishes, you will find me to be patient.' So when they had both surrendered [to Allah's will], and he had laid him down on his forehead, We called out to him, 'O Abraham! You have indeed fulfilled your vision! Thus indeed do We reward the virtuous! This was indeed a manifest test.'[9]

It was through his patience in this 'manifest test' that Abraham was able to attain the status of imamate. In another verse God says,

وَجَعَلْنَا مِنْهُمْ أَئِمَّةً يَهْدُونَ بِأَمْرِنَا لَمَّا صَبَرُوا وَكَانُوا بِآيَاتِنَا يُوقِنُونَ

When they had been patient and had certainty in Our signs, We appointed amongst them imams to guide [the people] by Our command.[10]

This tells us that there are two conditions for the status of imamate: patience in a manifest test and a distinct spiritual station referred to as certainty in God's signs. How is this certainty attained?

وَاعْبُدْ رَبَّكَ حَتَّىٰ يَأْتِيَكَ الْيَقِينُ

Worship your Lord until certainty comes to you.[11]

This type of patience and worship allow the individual to rise to the position of the imam– a position where they become a role model worthy of being followed.[12] In fact, this patience and worship grants the individual the quality of immaculacy that allows them to become imams. As God says,

أَفَمَن يَهْدِي إِلَى الْحَقِّ أَحَقُّ أَن يُتَّبَعَ أَمَّن لَّا يَهِدِّي إِلَّا أَن يُهْدَىٰ

Is He who guides to the truth worthier to be followed, or he who is not guided unless shown the way?[13]

People who are in need of guidance are not worthy of being followed. Would you rather take the advice of an experienced surgeon or a

---

[9] The Holy Qur'an, 37:101-06.

[10] The Holy Qur'an, 32:24.

[11] The Holy Qur'an, 15:99.

[12] This type of worship does not stop when an individual reaches certainty and the station of imamate. The Prophet Muḥammad was already certain, but the Lord addressed him in this verse nonetheless. God prescribed for the Prophet a perpetual state of closeness to Him. Even an individual with the highest degree of spiritual certainty should continue to worship in order to draw to an even more profound level of sincerity, such that the person continues to worship God sincerely until they face the certainty of death.

[13] The Holy Qur'an, 10:35.

medical student? The same applies in the realm of divine guidance. Only those who reached the status of being perfect role models are truly worthy of being followed. The individuals that hold this status must be above any doubt or criticism.[14] That is why God describes these individuals saying,

إِنَّمَا يُرِيدُ اللَّهُ لِيُذْهِبَ عَنكُمُ الرِّجْسَ أَهْلَ الْبَيْتِ وَيُطَهِّرَكُمْ تَطْهِيرًا

Indeed Allah desires to repel all impurity from you, O People of the Household, and purify you with a thorough purification.[15]

Constancy of the Imam

Reading through the Qur'anic verses, we can also begin to see imamate as a core and constant concept. Continuously throughout the ages, God appointed imams to fulfill this grand role. He says in His Holy Book,

إِنَّا نَحْنُ نُحْيِي الْمَوْتَىٰ وَنَكْتُبُ مَا قَدَّمُوا وَآثَارَهُمْ ۚ وَكُلَّ شَيْءٍ أَحْصَيْنَاهُ فِي إِمَامٍ مُّبِينٍ

Indeed it is We who revive the dead and write what they have sent ahead and their effects [which they left behind], and We have figured everything in a manifest imam.[16]

And speaking of the Day of Judgement, the Holy Qur'an says,

يَوْمَ نَدْعُو كُلَّ أُنَاسٍ بِإِمَامِهِمْ

The day We shall summon every group of people along with their imam....[17]

An imam is present for every people throughout time, witnessing their actions and serving as God's proof amongst them. As we read in a verse cited earlier,

إِنَّمَا أَنتَ مُنذِرٌ ۖ وَلِكُلِّ قَوْمٍ هَادٍ

You are only a warner, and there is a guide for every people.[18]

---

[14] A prophet or imam must be above any doubt or criticism for several reasons. First, to be perfect role models, they must be perfect in every sense. They must not fall prey to any error, intentional or not. Second, if they are individuals in whom God asked us to place our absolute faith and confidence, there can be no room for doubt. They must therefore be free of any error, intentional or not. Third, individuals who are appointed by God to act as guardians of His message must be able to do so at all times and circumstances. This entails that they are free of all errors, intentional or not.

[15] The Holy Qur'an, 33:33.

[16] The Holy Qur'an, 36:12.

[17] The Holy Qur'an, 17:71.

[18] The Holy Qur'an, 13:7.

We can thus see that there is a continuum of imamate throughout time. However, there are certain points of emphasis that we see in the holy verses and noble traditions. Qur'anically, we see an emphasis with Abraham who was made an imam after having passed that manifest test. The Holy Qur'an tells us that Abraham would supplicate to his Lord and say,

رَبِّ هَبْ لِي حُكْمًا وَأَلْحِقْنِي بِالصَّالِحِينَ ۞ وَاجْعَل لِّي لِسَانَ صِدْقٍ فِي الْآخِرِينَ

My Lord! Grant me [unerring] judgement, and unite me with the Righteous. Confer on me a worthy repute among the posterity.[19]

Amongst the other verses we recounted of Abraham's story, we find that God's chosen servants would supplicate to Him and ask,

وَالَّذِينَ يَقُولُونَ رَبَّنَا هَبْ لَنَا مِنْ أَزْوَاجِنَا وَذُرِّيَّاتِنَا قُرَّةَ أَعْيُنٍ وَاجْعَلْنَا لِلْمُتَّقِينَ إِمَامًا

And those who say, 'Our Lord! Give us joy and comfort in our spouses and offspring, and make us imams of the Godwary.'[20]

God answered Abraham's prayers and granted him and his descendants that lofty status.

وَوَهَبْنَا لَهُم مِّن رَّحْمَتِنَا وَجَعَلْنَا لَهُمْ لِسَانَ صِدْقٍ عَلِيًّا

And We gave them out of Our mercy, and conferred on them a worthy and lofty repute.[21]

God did not only make Abraham an imam, but answered his supplication and gave that lofty status to the chosen amongst his descendants – the greatest of whom is our beloved Holy Prophet Muḥammad. That is why our Prophet said in the noble tradition,

أنا دعوة أبي إبراهيم

I am the [answered] prayer of my father Abraham.[22]

God gave His chosen servants this status and promised them that one day they will inherit the Earth.

وَلَقَدْ كَتَبْنَا فِي الزَّبُورِ مِن بَعْدِ الذِّكْرِ أَنَّ الْأَرْضَ يَرِثُهَا عِبَادِيَ الصَّالِحُونَ

---

[19] The Holy Qur'an, 26:83-84.

[20] The Holy Qur'an, 25:74.

[21] The Holy Qur'an, 19:50.

[22] al-Ṣadūq, *Man lā yahdhuruh al-faqīh*, 2:379.

> *Certainly We wrote in the Psalms, after the Reminder: 'Indeed My righteous servants shall inherit the Earth.'*[23]

In this grand narrative of imamate, there is a crucial turning point to which we must turn our attention. We read in the visitation of our Holy Prophet,

اَلسَّلامُ عَلَى رَسُولِ اللهِ أَمِينِ اللهِ عَلَى وَحْيِهِ وَعَزائِمِ اَمْرِهِ الْخَاتِمِ لِمَا سَبَقَ وَالْفَاتِحِ لِمَا اسْتُقْبِلَ وَالْمُهَيْمِنِ عَلَى ذٰلِكَ كُلِّهِ

> *Peace be upon the Messenger of God, the Trustee of God over His revelations and the weightiest of His commands – the seal of what had passed, the harbinger of what was to come, and the master over it all!* [24]

If we look at religious history before the time of our Holy Prophet, we see that it centered around prophets and messengers. God sealed that phase of human development with His beloved Prophet. A new phase of history began with religious leaders – imams – at its center. Yet he was not simply that turning point in history. His light emanated throughout the history of creation. It was his name and names of his family that were taught to Adam, and through those names the progenitor of humanity found forgiveness for his shortcoming.[25] The noble traditions tell us that God established a covenant with every prophet that they believe in this final messenger and prepare their people for that day. Prophet Jesus would declare to his people,

إِنِّي رَسُولُ اللَّهِ إِلَيْكُم مُّصَدِّقًا لِّمَا بَيْنَ يَدَيَّ مِنَ التَّوْرَاةِ وَمُبَشِّرًا بِرَسُولٍ يَأْتِي مِن بَعْدِي اسْمُهُ أَحْمَدُ

> *Indeed I am the apostle of Allah to you, to confirm what is before me of the Torah, and to give the good news of an apostle who will come after me, whose name is Aḥmad.*[26]

This allows us to understand their pivotal role in the world of creation. As we read in *al-Ziyārah al-jāmiʿah al-kabīrah*,

خَلَقَكُمُ اللهُ أَنْوَاراً فَجَعَلَكُمْ بِعَرْشِهِ مُحَدِّقِينَ حَتَّى مَنَّ عَلَيْنَا بِكُمْ فَجَعَلَكُمْ فِي بُيُوتٍ أَذِنَ اللهُ أَنْ تُرْفَعَ وَيُذْكَرَ فِيهَا اسْمُهُ

---

[23] The Holy Qurʾan, 21:105.
[24] al-Qummī, *Mafātīḥ al-jinān*, 366.
[25] See: Arastu, *God's Emissaries*, 48-49.
[26] The Holy Qurʾan, 61:6.

Allah created you as lights and kept you closely attached with His Throne until He, out of His favor, bestowed you upon us – placing you in houses that He allowed to be elevated and for His name to be mentioned therein.[27]

With this great gift, God Almighty gave the righteous amongst the Muslim ummah a lofty status amongst all others. It allowed that community to be witnesses upon all other nations. God says in the Holy Qur'an,

وَكَذَٰلِكَ جَعَلْنَاكُمْ أُمَّةً وَسَطًا لِّتَكُونُوا شُهَدَاءَ عَلَى النَّاسِ وَيَكُونَ الرَّسُولُ عَلَيْكُمْ شَهِيدًا

Thus We have made you a middle ummah that you may be witnesses to the people, and that the Apostle may be a witness to you.[28]

DIVINE DOMINION AND IMAMATE

When we read the verses pertaining to imamate and guidance, we find that God makes it conditional upon His command. For example, He says,

وَجَعَلْنَاهُمْ أَئِمَّةً يَهْدُونَ بِأَمْرِنَا وَأَوْحَيْنَا إِلَيْهِمْ فِعْلَ الْخَيْرَاتِ وَإِقَامَ الصَّلَاةِ وَإِيتَاءَ الزَّكَاةِ ۖ وَكَانُوا لَنَا عَابِدِينَ

We made them imams, guiding by Our command, and We revealed to them the performance of good deeds, the maintenance of prayers, and the giving of zakat, and they used to worship Us.[29]

What does God mean when He speaks of His command? We find that in another verse He says,

أَلَا لَهُ الْخَلْقُ وَالْأَمْرُ

All creation and command belong to Him.[30]

He also says,

إِنَّمَا أَمْرُهُ إِذَا أَرَادَ شَيْئًا أَن يَقُولَ لَهُ كُن فَيَكُونُ ۞ فَسُبْحَانَ الَّذِي بِيَدِهِ مَلَكُوتُ كُلِّ شَيْءٍ وَإِلَيْهِ تُرْجَعُونَ

---

[27] al-Qummī, *Mafātīḥ al-jinān*, 551.

[28] The Holy Qur'an, 2:143. The Holy Qur'an, 2:143. This lofty status is not meant for the entire ummah, but specifically for the righteous within it. For more, see the exegesis of the verse in al-Ṭabāṭabā'ī's *al-Mīzān*.

[29] The Holy Qur'an, 21:73.

[30] The Holy Qur'an, 7:54.

> *All His command, when He wills something, is to say to it 'Be,' and it is. So glory be to Him in whose hand is the dominion of all things, and to whom you shall be brought back.*[31]

From these verses we understand that God's commands go beyond the typical system of causes and effects in the natural world. They are effectuated through God's ultimate dominion over all things – His *malakūt.*

So imamate is the role of guidance by God's commands, which comes through this system of His dominion.

Reading further into the verses we see that God conditions granting this role and status on the individual's certitude. He says,

وَجَعَلْنَا مِنْهُمْ أَئِمَّةً يَهْدُونَ بِأَمْرِنَا لَمَّا صَبَرُوا ۖ وَكَانُوا بِآيَاتِنَا يُوقِنُونَ

> *When they had been patient and had certainty in Our signs, We appointed amongst them imams to guide [the people] by Our command.*[32]

In another verse He says,

وَكَذَٰلِكَ نُرِي إِبْرَاهِيمَ مَلَكُوتَ السَّمَاوَاتِ وَالْأَرْضِ وَلِيَكُونَ مِنَ الْمُوقِنِينَ

> *Thus did We show Abraham the dominion of the heavens and the Earth, that he might be of those who possess certitude.*[33]

How does someone attain this certitude? The Holy Qur'an says,

وَاعْبُدْ رَبَّكَ حَتَّىٰ يَأْتِيَكَ الْيَقِينُ

> *Worship your Lord until certainty comes to you.*[34]

What are the characteristics of this servitude? God says,

إِنَّا أَنزَلْنَا إِلَيْكَ الْكِتَابَ بِالْحَقِّ فَاعْبُدِ اللَّهَ مُخْلِصًا لَّهُ الدِّينَ

> *Indeed We have sent down the Book to you with the truth; so worship Allah, putting exclusive faith in Him.*[35]

We find that the Holy Qur'an places great emphasis on devotion in worship, especially when speaking of His greatest servants. Through devoted worship, an individual can attain certainty. And to better understand certainty, let us turn again to the Holy Qur'an.

---

31 The Holy Qur'an, 36:82-83.

32 The Holy Qur'an, 32:24.

33 The Holy Qur'an, 6:75.

34 The Holy Qur'an, 15:99.

35 The Holy Qur'an, 39:2.

كَلَّا لَوْ تَعْلَمُونَ عِلْمَ الْيَقِينِ ۞ لَتَرَوُنَّ الْجَحِيمَ

Indeed, were you to know with certain knowledge, you would have surely seen Hell [in this very life].[36]

This is one type of certainty. God speaks of another type of certainty that leads to the opposite end.

وَجَحَدُوا بِهَا وَاسْتَيْقَنَتْهَا أَنفُسُهُمْ

They denied it, though they were convinced in their hearts.[37]

There is a difference between these two certainties mentioned in the Holy Qur'an. The latter type mentioned is one built on acquired knowledge (*al-ʿilm al-muktasab*) and thus is still prone to error. The former is presential knowledge (*al-ʿilm al-ḥuḍūrī*) that cannot be altered or erased.[38] It is the former type that is a precondition of attaining imamate. We will address certainty in further detail elsewhere in this book.

We can thus see an intricate relationship between worship and patience, certainty and perseverance, divine dominion and command, and guidance as the role of the imam.

---

36 The Holy Qur'an, 102:5-6.

37 The Holy Qur'an, 27:14.

38 Acquired and presential knowledge are addressed in detail in the next chapter.

ON KNOWLEDGE AND AUTHORITY

ʿAllāmah Naṣīr al-Dīn al-Ṭūsī (d. 672/1274) categorized knowledge into four levels. He explained his categorization with an allegory like this:

Imagine a blind caveman who knows nothing about fire. He lacks any type of knowledge about what fire is and what it is used for. How does he come to know fire?

At the most basic level, our caveman can begin to learn about fire through the words and testimony of others. We can begin to explain to him its properties and uses – how it generates light and heat, and how we can use it to cook a meal. At this level, all his knowledge of fire comes through whatever evidence his peers can provide and teach him. He might accept or reject whatever ideas others present to him, depending on how convincing and trustworthy he finds them.

We offer our caveman a nice hot meal that we cooked using fire. His experience of one of the effects of fire becomes proof for him that fire does in fact exist. This is a higher form of knowledge that rests on evidence. However, with this form of knowledge, there is still a distance between the knowledge and the object of that knowledge. Experiencing the effect, although it is evidence of the cause, is not a direct experience of the cause.

We can bring our caveman closer to the fire so that he can feel its warmth, hear its crackles, and smell its smoke. These repeated sensory experiences of the fire and its effects give him certainty of its existence. So much so that they will leave him with no room to doubt or forget fire's reality. However, there is still room for error in his understanding of fire. He might come across the smoke of a smoldering log and mistake it for a fire. Or he might deny the existence of a fire when he doesn't hear a crackle.

The highest level of knowledge will come to him when he puts his hand in the fire. The sensation of the fire burning his hands will not only impress sensory experiences on him but will also bring that pain – if not the fire itself – to be present within him. This presential knowledge is not only undoubtable and unforgettable while being experienced consciously, but it is also free of any possibility of error.[1] This type of knowledge is much more immediate. An individual can never make a mistake about things that are present within themselves such as whether or not they are in pain.

To draw a more realistic example, think of an individual's understanding of death. At a young age, a child only knows about death as an idea. He has heard that people who once were alive are no longer so. At some point in his life, a friend's family member might pass away. Hearing about the deceased and seeing the effects of his passing on the family will elevate the child's understanding of death. As this child grows, so will his family and loved ones. At some point, the individual will lose a family member. Then maybe a friend. Seeing his own loved ones pass away will once again elevate his knowledge of death. Then at some point he will himself pass on. Death will become his reality, which he cannot mistake or deny.

This order of knowledge helps us better conceptualize what it means to know or have certainty. ʿAllāmah al-Ṭūsī says that the third tier (i.e., seeing the fire) is the lowest level of certainty as addressed in the Holy Qurʾan. As the holy verse describes,

كَلَّا لَوْ تَعْلَمُونَ عِلْمَ الْيَقِينِ ۝ لَتَرَوُنَّ الْجَحِيمَ

[1] Presential knowledge cannot err so long as an individual's mind remains sound. Even if a person is not of sound mind, how can we doubt whether they feel pain? Errors can occur in remembering, communicating, or building on such knowledge. If I am in pain, no one can tell me that I'm wrong about the pain I feel. I may err in remembering a previous pain, communicating the pain I feel, or diagnosing the underlying cause – all of which are forms of acquired knowledge and therefore subject to error.

Indeed, were you to know with certain knowledge, you would have surely seen Hell [in this very life].[2]

When the Holy Qur'an and the noble traditions speak of the certainty attained by God's closest servants, they refer to the highest level that comes with presential knowledge. We can see this from the words of our Immaculate Imams about certainty. Imam ʿAlī said,

مَا شَكَكْتُ فِي الْحَقِّ مُذْ أُرِيتُهُ

I did not doubt the Truth [i.e., God] since I was shown it.[3]

This is the level of certainty that Imam al-Ḥusayn teaches us to have in his famous supplication for the Day of ʿArafah. He said,

أَيَكُونُ لِغَيْرِكَ مِنَ ٱلظُّهُورِ مَا لَيْسَ لَكَ حَتَّىٰ يَكُونَ هُوَ ٱلْمُظْهِرَ لَكَ ؟ مَتَىٰ غِبْتَ حَتَّىٰ تَحْتَاجَ إِلَىٰ دَلِيلٍ يَدُلُّ عَلَيْكَ ؟ وَمَتَىٰ بَعُدْتَ حَتَّىٰ تَكُونَ ٱلآثَارُ هِيَ ٱلَّتِي تُوصِلُ إِلَيْكَ ؟ عَمِيَتْ عَيْنٌ لاَ تَرَاكَ عَلَيْهَا رَقِيباً!

Can anything other than You hold any kind of manifestation that You lack so that it may reveal You? When have You ever been absent so that You may need something to point to You? When have You ever been far-off so that traces may lead to You? Blind is an eye that cannot see You watching it! [4]

Acquired and Presential Knowledge

It is important to distinguish here between presential and acquired knowledge (*al-ʿilm al-ḥuḍūrī wa'l-ʿilm al-ḥuṣūlī*). Our scholars lay out the distinction between these two types of knowledge in their works on logic and philosophy.[5]

Scholars define presential knowledge as the presence of the subject itself to the knower. Acquired knowledge, on the other hand, comes through the acquisition of mental images of the object. How does an individual know pain? This is a very common example given to illustrate the difference between acquired and presential knowledge. An individual may know pain by people's description of it. He might remember a time when he was hurt and felt that pain. He might see another individual in pain and extract a mental impression or draw a mental image of

[2] The Holy Qur'an, 102:5-6.

[3] al-Raḍī, *Nahj al-balāghah*, Short Saying 184.

[4] al-Qummī, *Mafātīḥ al-jinān*, 298.

[5] For example, see ʿAllāmah Ṭabāṭabā'ī, *The Elements of Islamic Metaphysics*, 153–55.

what that individual may be feeling. But no one knows pain like the individual who was in pain at the moment. The pain itself is present to that individual. Its presence leads to several effects such as discomfort and groaning.

The former type of knowledge is acquired, while the latter is presential. Recognizing this distinction allows us to identify some of the properties of each type of knowledge.

Because presential knowledge comes through the presence of the subject to the knower, it does not need any sort of intermediary to communicate it to the mind. Conversely, acquired knowledge must come through a medium – what we referred to earlier as mental images. Think of a tree. That tree does not actually exist in your mind. What is in your mind is only an image of a reality that exists outside your mind that you extracted from your sense perception.

However, this intermediary is prone to error. An error in the senses, for example, could create a mental image that does not correspond to reality. A colorblind individual may create a mental image of a green sign, when the sign is in reality red.

The fact that presential knowledge does not rely on such an intermediary means that it is not prone to error. The subject matter and the individual's knowledge of it are one and the same with presential knowledge – there is no room for any discrepancy, mistake or doubt

Knowledge and Reason

We can now see that there are some forms of knowledge that are inseparably attached to truth. Although we recognize much of our knowledge as prone to error, there are times when error is simply an impossibility. As we saw with presential knowledge, there is no room for any error because the reality of the subject and the individual's knowledge of it are one and the same. This is also the case with the most intuitive premises we start off with in our thinking, and with our soundly argued conclusions, so long as we are systematically careful and attentive throughout the argumentation.[6]

[6] The principle of non-contradiction is the primary example of a self-evident intuitive premise. We can neither provide a prove for this axiom, nor can we falsify it in any way. Moreover, all proofs rely on it as a prior assumption. This and similar examples are studied in detail in the books of epistemology and logic.

This allows us to understand with more depth some of the noble traditions concerning reason and its role in the world of creation. If we look at the book of *al-Kāfī*, we find that al-Shaykh al-Kulaynī lists the following tradition from Imam al-Bāqir as the very first tradition in his encyclopedia:

لما خلق الله العقل استنطقه ثم قال له: أقبل فأقبل ثم قال له: أدبر فأدبر ثم قال: وعزتي وجلالي ما خلقت خلقا هو أحب إلي منك ولا أكملتك إلا فيمن أحب، أما إني إياك آمر، وإياك أنهى وإياك أعاقب، وإياك أثيب.

> *When God created reason, He commanded it to speak. He then said to it 'come' and it came forth. He said to it 'go' and it went forth. He then said, 'By My honor and glory, I have not created anything more beloved to me than you, nor shall I perfect you in anyone except those whom I love! Indeed, it is you that I command, you that I forbid, you that I punish, and you that I reward.'* [7]

By virtue of its creation, reason is infallible. So long as it is the faculty dictating an individual's actions, he will not fall into any mistake. The problem – as we've addressed previously – lies in all the other faculties that aim to subvert reason and use it for their purposes. If an individual is able to subdue all these other faculties and act on pure reason, he will have no room for error. Sound and pure reason unhindered by the passions always judges correctly.

Why did God create us with these subversive faculties? Why did He not just endow us with pure reason and allow us to be free from all mistakes? In His ultimate wisdom, God did create a set of beings with those characteristics – beings of light that we generally refer to as angels. God endowed the angels with pure reason and no subversive faculties so that they may worship and glorify Him. Yet God had a different plan for humanity.

وَإِذْ قَالَ رَبُّكَ لِلْمَلَائِكَةِ إِنِّي جَاعِلٌ فِي الْأَرْضِ خَلِيفَةً ۖ قَالُوا أَتَجْعَلُ فِيهَا مَنْ يُفْسِدُ فِيهَا وَيَسْفِكُ الدِّمَاءَ وَنَحْنُ نُسَبِّحُ بِحَمْدِكَ وَنُقَدِّسُ لَكَ ۖ قَالَ إِنِّي أَعْلَمُ مَا لَا تَعْلَمُونَ

> *When your Lord said to the angels, 'Indeed I am going to set a viceroy on the earth,' they said, 'Will You set in it someone who will cause corruption in it and shed blood, while we celebrate*

[7] al-Kulaynī, *al-Kāfī*, 1:10.

> *Your praise and proclaim Your sanctity?' He said, 'Indeed I know what you do not know.'* [8]

When God told the angels of this new creation – one that possessed both reason and the other faculties – they recognized that such beings are prone to error. In fact, they figured that humanity will commit great atrocities when the base faculties overcome reason. Yet God's answer to their inquiries was clear – He knew that there was amongst this creation a group that would subordinate their base faculties to pure reason. God created this new species because he knew that such individuals would rise to the occasion. In fact, He created the whole of creation for the sake of these individuals who would embody pure reason by their free will and against all odds. Such individuals rise above the rank of the infallible angels, as they act with the same reason, but only after overcoming great trials.

Thus, through the exercise of reason huamnity can become greater than the angels. As Imam ʿAlī said,

> إن الله ركب في الملائكة عقلا بلا شهوة، وركب في البهائم شهوة بلا عقل، وركب في بني آدم كليهما، فمن غلب عقله شهوته فهو خير من الملائكة، ومن غلبت شهوته عقله فهو شر من البهائم.
>
> *God instilled in angels reason without desire, instilled in beasts desire without reason, and instilled both in the children of Adam. Surely, whoever allows his reason to overcome his desire is greater than the angels, and whoever allows his desire to overcome his reason is more wretched than the beasts.* [9]

Pure reason is infallible by its nature. Knowledge comes in many shapes, including certain types of knowledge that are objectively immune to error. This combination of pure reason and inerrant knowledge allows an individual to rise in status and claim the positions of prophethood and imamate. How? By their immaculate nature, both reason and inerrant knowledge allow the individual to exhibit the characteristics that we see in our imams.

This level of inerrant knowledge allowed Imam ʿAlī to see the truth with such certainty that he can say,

> لو كشف لي الغطاء ما ازددت يقيناً

[8] The Holy Qur'an, 2:30.

[9] al-Ṣadūq, *ʿIlal al-sharāʾiʿ*, 1:12.

If the veil [of reality] were lifted for me, I would not increase in certitude! [10]

He had no misgivings about his own knowledge and faith. He possessed such immense knowledge, yet we see his humility when he hears the name of the greatest of creations, the Holy Prophet. A man once asked him, "When was your Lord?" The Imam replied,

ثَكِلَتْكَ أُمُّكَ، وَ مَتَى لَمْ يَكُنْ حَتَّى يُقَالَ مَتَى كَانَ، كَانَ رَبِّي قَبْلَ الْقَبْلِ بِلَا قَبْلٍ، وَ بَعْدَ الْبَعْدِ بِلَا بَعْدٍ وَلَا غَايَةَ وَ لَا مُنْتَهَى لِغَايَتِهِ، انْقَطَعَتِ الْغَايَاتُ عِنْدَهُ فَهُوَ مُنْتَهَى كُلِّ غَايَةٍ

May your mother grieve for you! When was He not so that it can be asked 'when was He'? My Lord was before beforeness with nothing before and after afterness with nothing after and no [maximum] extent. There is no end to His extent. All aims end with Him, for He is the [ultimate] end of every aim.

The questioner was so amazed by his answer that he blurted, "Are you a prophet?" He responded,

وَيْلَكَ، إِنَّمَا أَنَا عَبْدٌ مِنْ عَبِيدِ مُحَمَّدٍ

Woe to you! Rather, I am a servant from amongst the servants of Muḥammad! [11]

KNOWLEDGE AND AUTHORITY

This particular knowledge we have been speaking of – special in quantity and quality – grants its holder a lofty status that comes with a number of specific products. The Holy Qur'an makes mention of this type of knowledge and authority when it relays the story of Prophet Solomon. When the Queen of Sheba was heading to meet him, he asked his courtiers to perform an extraordinary feat.

قَالَ يَا أَيُّهَا الْمَلَأُ أَيُّكُمْ يَأْتِينِي بِعَرْشِهَا قَبْلَ أَن يَأْتُونِي مُسْلِمِينَ ۞ قَالَ عِفْرِيتٌ مِّنَ الْجِنِّ أَنَا آتِيكَ بِهِ قَبْلَ أَن تَقُومَ مِن مَّقَامِكَ ۖ وَإِنِّي عَلَيْهِ لَقَوِيٌّ أَمِينٌ ۞ قَالَ الَّذِي عِندَهُ عِلْمٌ مِّنَ الْكِتَابِ أَنَا آتِيكَ بِهِ قَبْلَ أَن يَرْتَدَّ إِلَيْكَ طَرْفُكَ ۚ فَلَمَّا رَآهُ مُسْتَقِرًّا عِندَهُ قَالَ هَٰذَا مِن فَضْلِ رَبِّي

He said, 'O [members of the] elite! Which of you will bring me her throne before they come to me in submission?' An ʿifrīt from among the jinn said, 'I will bring it to you before you rise from

10 al-Wāṣiṭī, *ʿUyūn al-ḥikam*, 415.

11 al-Kulaynī, *al-Kāfī*, 1:89.

your place. I have the power to do it and am trustworthy.' The one who had some knowledge of the Book said, 'I will bring it to you in the twinkling of an eye.' So when he saw it set near him, he said, 'This is by the grace of my Lord....' [12]

It was Solomon's viceroy who had 'some knowledge of the Book' that was able to perform that extraordinary task. If a piece of that knowledge gave him this kind of ability, what would knowledge of the entire Book allow him? In another verse we read,

كَفَىٰ بِاللَّهِ شَهِيدًا بَيْنِي وَبَيْنَكُمْ وَمَنْ عِندَهُ عِلْمُ الْكِتَابِ

Allah suffices as a witness between me and you, and he who possesses the knowledge of the Book.[13]

The one who possesses 'the knowledge of the Book' is elevated to the status of witness upon God's creation. This is just one of the distinctions allowed to those who hold this knowledge, alongside the others such as immaculacy and *al-Wilāyah al-Takwīniyyah*, or creational authority.[14] And if Solomon's viceroy held some knowledge of the Book, the imams from the Holy Household possessed it all. As Imam al-Ṣādiq said,

علم الكتاب والله كله عندنا

By God, the entirety of the knowledge of the Book is with us![15]

In addition, an imam's possession of this particular knowledge grants him the authority to guide by God's command. God says in the Holy Qur'an,

وَجَعَلْنَا مِنْهُمْ أَئِمَّةً يَهْدُونَ بِأَمْرِنَا لَمَّا صَبَرُوا وَكَانُوا بِآيَاتِنَا يُوقِنُونَ

---

[12] The Holy Qur'an, 27:38-40.

[13] The Holy Qur'an, 13:43.

[14] *al-wilāyah al-takwīniyyah*, translated here as 'creational authority,' is a privilege with which God graces some of His closest servants. The Arabic *takwīn* is derived from the root verb K-W-N (*kāf - wāw - nūn*), which means 'brought into being or existence.' Creational authority is the ability and liberty to affect the existence of any being. Such authority may be essential to its possessor, completely independent of any outside factors. This is the case with God Almighty's creational authority. Creational authority could also be held through delegation by a creature in their dependence upon the creator. Shia Muslims believe that prophets, messengers, and imams hold such authority by God's leave. For more, see: al-Khabbāz, *al-Wilāyah al-takwīniyyah*.

[15] al-Kulaynī, *al-Kāfī*, 1:257.

> *When they had been patient and had certainty in Our signs, We appointed amongst them imams to guide [the people] by Our command.*[16]

As we have discussed, Prophet Abraham was granted this status and ability after he passed his manifest trial. Yet we must ask, if Abraham was a prophet with the mission of guidance before he was appointed an imam, what is this new level of 'guidance by God's command' that was bestowed upon him? Keeping in mind the specific meaning of 'God's command' (briefly discussed in an earlier chapter), our scholars come to the following conclusion about an imam's ability to guide.

Our scholars say that prophethood comes with the duty to guide by showing a people the truth. God's prophets and messengers come as warners (*nathīr*) and heralds of good news (*bashīr*). Our scholars call this *al-hidāyah al-irāʾiyyah*, or guidance through demonstration. Being appointed to the position of imamate gives a greater ability for guidance – what our scholars call *al-hidāyah al-iyṣāliyyah*, or guidance by deliverance, guidance of the follower all the way through arriving at the goal. An imam not only shows people the correct path but walks them through it to deliver them to their final destination. This is not a guidance that is imposed but is a product of the receptivity and free will of the one that is being guided.

Al-hidāyah al-iyṣāliyyah is guidance through divinely endowed charisma[17] – a sort of law of spiritual gravity. The knowledge attained by an imam provides a position of guidance where the hearts and minds of believers are drawn toward him. This allows them to draw the believers closer and lead them along the straight path, delivering them to the salvation they seek. An individual may follow the call of that spiritual gravity – the imams' *hidāyah iyṣāliyyah* – or may rebel against it. The imams have the power and authority to guide, yet the free will of every individual is preserved.

The reader should realize that, as the Qurʾanic verses show us, these concepts are at the heart of imamate. The issues of political power and governorship – though important and are part and parcel of imamate –

---

16 The Holy Qurʾan, 32:24.

17 Charisma is defined as "compelling attractiveness or charm that can inspire devotion in others" or "a divinely conferred power or talent." (*Oxford Dictionary*, s.v. "charisma"). The Latin roots of the word denotes divine grace and favor. Throughout this book, we used the term 'charisma' to refer to the imams' divinely endowed ability to attract people's hearts and spirits to them.

are not the core issues. The political role of the Imam can facilitate the accessibility of the Imam's knowledge and guidance, helping to advance individuals and communities. Still, imamate is a position that carries great existential value and cannot be reduced to a historical political dilemma. To do so is an injustice to our imams and a misunderstanding of their true divinely appointed role.

Temporal Power

An imam's power and duty to guide do not compel their followers. Just because the Imam has the authority and duty to guide does not mean that people lose their free will and choice. People must make their individual choices of whether they will follow this guidance. Yet each of us lives in a realm of constant conflict. We have described in detail the conflict between all the base faculties, and their collective conflict against reason. These faculties do not only exist on an individual level but are forces within society at large driving it in one direction or another. This conflicted space makes it difficult for the individual to make rational choices as opposed to choices dictated by gluttony, wrath, and the other faculties.

Therefore, there was a need for a temporal power – one with political, social, economic, and other worldly dimensions – to place restrictions on the excesses of these faculties. This would allow reason to make its choices within a more neutral environment.

Just as the imams' power of guidance does not compel their followers , neither is their temporal power meant to be so. Compulsion is, generally speaking, a rationally and morally disdained idea. Even during the brief periods where an immaculate exercised full political power and authority, they did not force their citizens to be perfect Muslims. In fact, no amount of political power can allow a governor to force citizens into absolute and perfect conformity.

Yet just as compulsion is a rationally and morally rejected idea, so is the idea of absolute and unlimited liberty which leads to lawlessness and anarchy. Political philosophers have theorized about how human society would look if there were no laws or governments limiting each individual's ability to act freely in their self-interest. The result – they theorized – is a state of absolute anarchy where every individual is in a state of constant war with everyone else.[18] This is not the type of society where anyone would want to live.

So, if we can have neither absolute compulsion nor absolute liberty, there must be a middle balance to solve the dilemma.

How can this balanced space be created? Theoretically, it can be created through law. One prime example of this can be seen in Islamic teachings regarding trade and business. On the one end, Muslims are prohibited from seeking monetary gains by immoral means. This is the basis for the prohibition of usury. There are numerous verses in the Holy Qur'an that also prohibit deception and fraud. But Islam did not stop at pronouncing prohibitions. It also elucidated the legal avenues through which a Muslim can earn a livelihood. Our scholars have dedicated volumes to these studies. The Holy Qur'an eloquently summarized the whole point in the blessed verse,

قَالُوا إِنَّمَا الْبَيْعُ مِثْلُ الرِّبَا ۗ وَأَحَلَّ اللَّهُ الْبَيْعَ وَحَرَّمَ الرِّبَا

> *They say, 'Trade is just like usury.' While Allah has allowed trade and forbidden usury.*[19]

The law is not meant simply to compel a given action. Its purpose is to give everyone a fair opportunity to exercise their rational will. The duty of temporal power is to put the law in practical application in order to create a neutral environment for all, where all can make and pursue their choices away from excess influence by any force. This is an image of social justice that contemporary societies aim to achieve.

To better understand this concept, simply look at the most economically disadvantaged cities in contemporary societies. These cities are also the ones with the highest level of crime. Why? It is because these populations live in an environment where the excesses of the base faculties are allowed to take control. When fear and hunger are constant themes in a given population, their individual choices are severely restricted. It is the duty of a government to provide the mechanisms – through social welfare, educational, and other policies – that create a neutral environment where they are free to make their choices.

---

[18] See, for example: Hobbes, *Leviathan*, 183–88. Other philosophers who did not frame the issue in as extreme terms as Hobbes still provide a framework where there is some constraint on individuals' liberty.

[19] The Holy Qur'an, 2:275.

Power and Authority

The stated objective of contemporary governments is the establishment of social justice for their citizens. They do so by enacting and enforcing laws that they see befitting to that end. These choices may or may not advance the end goal, but the goal remains the same – to give everyone a fair chance and allow them the freedom of choice without excessive external influence.

A government that seeks to reach that goal does not simply enact and enforce laws about individual behavior. It utilizes a comprehensive system that can bring about that social justice in all spheres. A government is not just a force to police the actions of its citizens. It is a system that seeks justice in terms of education, social welfare, environmental quality, and other issues pertinent to the lives of its citizens.

So how does this understanding of government fit within a religious worldview? One that seeks not only to establish social justice, but cosmic justice as well. When there is an individual as we have described – an imam that possesses the trait of immaculacy, special knowledge, and the authority to guide by God's command – is there any reason to place anyone else at the head of state? Is there any individual more qualified than him? The rational answer is a resounding no.

Why should an individual follow any type of authority? If we attempt to derive a standard from the conduct of reasonable individuals around us, we can see that people reasonably follow an authority when that authority possesses a level of expertise and integrity. Take, for example, the authority of a doctor. An individual will take a doctor's advice if he knows that the doctor has the training and experience to be able to give sound advice. The individual will also take the advice if he knows that the doctor has the integrity not to misuse his position. If we know that the doctor has a monetary interest in the medical testing facility next door, we will be more skeptical about whether we actually need that test.

This is the same principle that we put forward more than a millennium ago. Legitimate authority is not about force. It is not obtained through military power or haphazard birthright traditions. The position of leadership is very significant and must have its proper qualifications. Only the most qualified substantively and morally should take that position so that they do not misuse or abuse their temporal power, and so that they maximize the efficiency of their office.

QUALIFICATIONS

We do not need to go further than the narrations in praise of Imam ʿAlī and the remainder of the Holy Household in order to establish their qualifications for the job. No one can claim to be superior, or even equal, to them. The revolt against their authority had no legitimacy.

This is by no means a radical view. Any fair review of history will lead the reader to this same conclusion. The simplest example is seen in the words of the second caliph who said, "If it were not for ʿAlī, ʿUmar would have perished!"[20] If Imam ʿAlī was so integral to the success of the Muslim ummah, why not allow him his rightful place?

Instead of allowing the imams to take their rightful place, a force came and sought to replace them. Not only was that force corrupt in itself, but it also corrupted society. That is why Imam Ḥusayn had no choice but to set out and seek to reform the ummah of his grandfather.

The meaning of caliphate began to dilute as time passed. At first, the rulers would call themselves the viceroys of the Holy Prophet, then the viceroys of God Himself! Yet everyone saw through their sham. Their empty words began to revive the Age of Ignorance (*al-jāhiliyyah*), although veiled in the image of Islam.[21] With time, that veil would also be thrown away so that what remained was a monarchy clearly built on worldly aims.

Take these few historical examples as evidence. The Sunni historian Ibn Kathīr (d. 774/1373) narrates that the Holy Prophet said,

الخلافة بعدي ثلاثون سنة ثم تكون ملكا

> *The caliphate after me is thirty years, then it shall become a monarchy.*[22]

As Ibn Kathīr explains, the period of the caliphate thus ended in the year 40 after Hijra with Imam Ḥasan's signing of the peace accord with Muʿāwiyah. Thus, once Muʿāwiyah came to the throne, the idea of a caliphate ended and the reign of the Umayyad monarchy began. As Muʿāwiyah himself said, "We have accepted it as a monarchy."[23]

---

20 Ibn ʿAbdulbar, *al-Istīʿāb*, 1103.

21 The Age of Ignorance refers to the period and the state of the Arabs before the advent of the mission of the Prophet Muḥammad.

22 Ibn Kathīr, *al-Bidāyah*, 5:221.

23 Ibid.

Ibn Ḥanbal recounts in his book *Faḍā ʾil al-ṣaḥābah*,

> *Saad ibn Malik entered the court of Mu ʿāwiyah and said, 'Peace be upon you, O' king!' Mu ʿāwiyah replied, 'And nothing else? You are the believers and I am your commander!' Saad said, 'That would be the case had we made you our commander!'*[24]

It is interesting to note the etymology of the word *malik* – or king – in the Arabic language. It does not only signify a single ruler, but also owner. It is a system where the king not only owns the land, but everyone and everything that walks on it. Are we expected to follow such individuals? Are we supposed to accept them as individuals of unquestionable authority? The position of rulership became so removed from Islam that a vile man like Yazīd ibn Muʿāwiyah ascended the throne without the slightest claim to legitimacy.

---

[24] Ibn Ḥanbal, *Faḍā ʾil al-ṣaḥābah*, 1:988.

ON RELIGIOUS AUTHORITY

We have seen thus far that the position of imamate qualifies its holder to be at the helm of any temporal power. We also saw from history that the imams from the Holy Household were not allowed to take their rightful place of leadership in this world. We must now ask; how did the imams operate once they were distanced from their rightful place? Did they isolate themselves from the rest of society? Did they consider it sufficient to work on an individual level as spiritual guides to their followers? Or did they continue to work on a large scale to lead the wider Muslim community?

Our understanding is that they worked both on an individual and a community level in order to fulfil their duty of guidance. In addition, they implemented a plan to foster a community within the larger Muslim ummah that would hold fast to their teachings and values. In doing so, they exercised temporal powers to the fullest extent they could under the circumstances. So much so that a nephew of Imam al-Kāẓim would directly report to the Abbasid ruler of the time, "I did not think that there were two caliphs in the world until I saw my uncle Mūsā ibn Jaʿfar [al-Kāẓim] being greeted as a caliph!"[1]

---

[1] Al-Kulaynī, *al-Kāfī*, 1:486.

Fostering the Righteous Community

Let us take a quick look at some of the factors that allowed the Holy Household to foster a community within the Muslim ummah carrying their teachings and values.

First, the imams' legitimacy was undeniable. They would constantly remind their followers that they are on the side of truth. This is seen in the well-known words of the Holy Prophet,

الحق مع علي وعلي مع الحق ولن يفترقا حتى يردا علي الحوض يوم القيامة

> *The truth is with Ali and Ali is with the truth. They will not separate until they reach me at the Pond [of Paradise] on the Day of Judgement.*[2]

Second, their tragic story played a great role in reinforcing this community. This is especially true for the tragic events related to Lady Fāṭimah and Imam Ḥusayn. These tragedies became pivotal moments of Muslim history, with their anniversaries commemorated annually. Commemorations of the injustice and oppression that they suffered thus became a hallmark of this community. And despite the many attempts to erase these commemorative rituals, they continue to be a point of unity for the followers of the Holy Household.

Third, they embodied the best moral values and virtues, and were above any reasonable form of critique. Despite having the propaganda of the empire targeted against them, there was no fault that can be found in them or used against them. Take the example of the Commander of the Faithful Imam ʿAlī who during Umayyad times was cursed on the pulpits throughout the Muslim ummah for decades. All this did not scratch Imam ʿAlī's immaculate record. Instead, it became a mark of disgrace on the Umayyads. Why? Because there was never an ounce of truth in the Umayyads' accusations and abuse.

The usurpers themselves could not deny this. On one occasion, the Abbasid Caliph al-Maʾmūn would turn to some of his companions and say, "Do you know who taught me Shiʿism?" They would answer, "No, by God, we do not know." He replied, "My father, al-Rashīd." Confused, his companions would ask, "How is that so when he ordered the killing of people

---

[2] Ibn ʿAsākir, *Tārīkh Dimashq*, 42:449; al-Majlisī, *Biḥār al-Anwār*, 38:38.

from that household?" Al-Maʾmūn replied, "He killed them in pursuit of power because power is vain."[3]

Al-Rashīd would honor Imam al-Kāẓim so greatly that al-Maʾmūn would be confounded and ask his father about his actions. To that al-Rashīd would reply, "My son, he is the possessor of the right [i.e., the caliphate or leadership]." Al-Maʾmūn then asked, "If you know that then why do you not return this right back to him?" Al-Rashīd would say, "It is power. By God, if you were to contest it with me, I would have your head..."[4]

Fourth, the Holy Household placed special attention on developing their followers in all spheres of their lives. They worked to ensure that their followers embodied the best of ethics and were of the best character, and also lead their communities in knowledge and status.

Imam Jaʿfar al-Ṣādiq would constantly remind his followers to be a good reflection on him and his forefathers. He would kindly advise them,

مَعَاشِرَ الشِّيعَةِ! كُونُوا لَنَا زَيْناً، وَلاَ تَكُونُوا عَلَيْنَا شَيْناً. قُولُوا لِلنَّاسِ حُسْناً، وَاحْفَظُوا أَلْسِنَتَكُمْ، وَكُفُّوهَا عَنِ الْفُضُولِ وَقُبْحِ الْقَوْلِ.

O [my] Shia! Be an adornment [i.e., a good reflection] for us and do not be a disgrace upon us. Speak kindly to people and guard your tongues, holding them from prying and abhorrent language.[5]

These teachings were not just words spoken by the imams but were put into practice by their followers. The respected Sunni scholar al-Jūzajānī would describe Shia scholars saying, "The most important narrators of Kufa... people tolerated them for their truthful tongues in narration" despite their differing ideology.[6]

These teachings allowed the followers of the Holy Household to survive and grow in a hostile environment. So long as the Shia continued to be upstanding citizens in their communities, they ensured the continuation and growth of their movement despite persecution.

Alongside ensuring the high moral standing of their followers, the imams also ensured their continued independence. They put great efforts in ensuring that this community had the knowledge it needed,

[3] al-Ḥasanī, *Sīrat al-aʾimmah al-ithnay ʿashar*, 2:330.

[4] Ibid.

[5] al-Ṭūsī, *al-Amālī*, 440.

[6] al-Jawzajānī, *Aḥwāl al-rijāl*, 123-24.

along with a corps of scholars to ensure their intellectual sufficiency. Imam al-Ṣādiq articulated this goal when he said,

لما حضرت أبي عليه السلام الوفاة قال: يا جعفر أوصيك بأصحابي خيرا، قلت: جعلت فداك والله لأدعنهم - والرجل منهم يكون في المصر - فلا يسأل أحدا

When death approached my father, he instructed me, 'O' Ja'far, I request you to take care of my companions.' I said, 'May I be your ransom! By God, I will leave them [with such knowledge that] they will not need to ask anyone in the land they are in.'[7]

This sowed the seed for the great level of scholarship that has continued to this day. It allowed for the continued advancement of our understanding of our faith. One clear example of this is this community's understanding of commemorative rituals. We find that Imam al-Ṣādiq would pray for the visitors of Imam al-Ḥusayn saying,

اللهم ان اعدائنا عابوا عليهم خروجهم فلم يمنعهم ذلك عن الشخوص إلينا، وخلافاً منهم على من خالفنا، فارحم تلك الوجوه التي قد غيرتها الشمس، وارحم تلك الخدود التي تقلبت على حفرة أبي عبدالله، وارحم تلك الأعين التي جرت دموعها رحمة لنا

God! Our enemies reproached them. However, it did not deter them from coming out for us to defy those that have defied us. God! Have mercy on the faces that were altered by the sun. Have mercy on the cheeks that roll over on the grave of Abū 'Abdullāh al-Ḥusayn. Have mercy on the eyes that shed tears for us.

The narrator, Mu'āwiyah ibn Wahab, relayed that he was so astounded by the Imam's prayer that he said,

May I be your ransom! If this prayer that I heard from you was for someone who does not know God Almighty, I would think that hellfire would never touch him! By God, I wish I would have visited him instead of performing Ḥajj!

The Imam asked Mu'āwiyah why he does not visit Imam al-Ḥusayn's grave more often. He responded, "I did not know that the matter was of this importance!" The Imam said,

يا معاوية من يدعو لزواره في السماء اكثر ممن يدعو لهم في الأرض

Mu'āwiyah! Those who pray for his visitors in the heavens are more than those who pray for them on the earth.[8]

---

[7] al-Kulaynī, *al-Kāfī*, 1:306.

[8] al-Qummī, *Kāmil al-ziyārāt*, 228-229.

Muʿāwiyah ibn Wahab, a close companion of Imam al-Ṣādiq did not understand the importance of visiting Imam al-Ḥusayn. Fast forward to this day. The importance of this visitation has become so well understood that very few will have any doubt about it. It has become so prevalent that millions will walk toward that tomb on the commemoration of Arbaʿīn.[9] This great advancement in the awareness that the Shia have of their faith came as the fruits of that seed laid long ago by our imams.

In addition to all this, the Holy Household ensured the economic independence of their followers so that they are not easily influenced by the ruling authorities. On countless occasions, they would stress the importance of earning a livelihood through trade and skilled labor. They instructed their followers on how religious dues should be spent in advancement of this cause. The independent institution of khums was a great advantage in this regard.

Through all this, the imams from the Holy Household were able to foster a community within the larger Muslim ummah that would carry on their teachings and values. This righteous community would hold fast to their way despite all hardships and persecution they would face.

It is important to note that the Holy Household worked hard to ensure that their followers would always be considered part of the wider Muslim community. They ensured that the Shia, although never a majority, were not cast outside the fold of Islam by political propaganda or by the tyranny of the masses. The Holy Household provided their followers with a strategy and an understanding of the faith that protected their lives and their identity and preserved their position within the wider Muslim community.

There are a few major teachings that we can point to in support of this point. For instance, the Holy Prophet, Imam ʿAlī, and the remainder of the imams, insisted that the title of 'Muslim' be ascribed to anyone who pronounces the *shahādatayn* – that there is no god but God and that Muḥammad is His messenger. Imam ʿAlī could have easily labeled his enemies disbelievers at the battles of Jamal, Ṣiffīn, and Nahrawān.[10] Demonizing the enemy in this way would have mobilized many in his

---

[9] *Arbaʿīn*, lit. the forty, is the commemoration mourning Imam al-Ḥusayn forty days after the day marking his martyrdom on ʿĀshūrā (10th Muḥarram) for which it has become a recommended custom and practice for devotees to visit his shrine in Karbala, often walking from distances for that purpose.

[10] For example, see: al-Hakeem, *Understanding Karbala*, 92-94.

support, but it would also have sacrificed his values and left critical long-term consequences on the Muslim ummah.

In addition, our imams taught us to preserve both our lives and our faith through the use of pious dissimulation, or *taqiyyah*. If professing one's faith meant a threat to the individual's life or livelihood, then our imams instructed us to keep our faith a secret. Moreover, they instructed us to live alongside our Muslim brothers and sisters with courtesy and civility. Imam al-Ṣādiq would instruct his followers,

> صِلُوا عَشَائِرَكُمْ، وَاشْهَدُوا جَنَائِزَهُمْ، وَعُودُوا مَرْضَاهُمْ، وَأَدُّوا حُقُوقَهُمْ؛ فَإِنَّ الرَّجُلَ مِنْكُمْ إِذَا وَرِعَ فِي دِينِهِ وَصَدَقَ الْحَدِيثَ وَأَدَّى الأَمَانَةَ وَحَسَّنَ خُلُقَهُ مَعَ النَّاسِ قِيلَ هَذَا جَعْفَرِيٌّ، فَيَسُرُّنِي ذَلِكَ وَيَدْخُلُ عَلَيَّ مِنْهُ السُّرُورَ، وَقِيلَ هَذَا أَدَبُ جَعْفَرٍ. وإِذَا كَانَ عَلَى غَيْرِ ذلِكَ دَخَلَ عَلَيَّ بَلَاؤُهُ وَعَارُهُ، وَقِيلَ هَذَا أَدَبُ جَعْفَرٍ.
>
> *Be in touch with your tribes, attend their funerals, visit their ill, and fulfill their rights. Surely, if a person amongst you was pious in his religion, truthful with his words, delivers the trusts [with which he was entrusted], and was well-mannered with the people, he would be called a Jaʿfarī. That would please me, and he would bring me great happiness. The people would say, 'These are the manners of Jaʿfar.' If a person was not like that, I would be saddened and ashamed by him, as they will then say, 'these are the manners of Jaʿfar.'*[11]

The imams even authorized their followers to take positions within their current governments, allowing them to serve the interests of the community and protect fellow community members from harm. Despite the fact that the position of political authority is the due right of the imams, they did not stop their followers from civic engagement and public service within the halls of power. One important example is that of ʿAlī ibn Yaqṭīn, a companion of Imam Mūsā al-Kāẓim. On several occasions, Imam al-Kāẓim would advise ʿAlī ibn Yaqṭīn to act in a specific manner so as to safeguard his job as a close minister of the caliph. When ʿAlī ibn Yaqṭīn was distraught by others' criticism of his work, Imam al-Kāẓim instructed him to remain in his position so that he may continue to serve his brothers.[12]

The Holy Household took a stand against the attempts at distorting the religion of Islam and misguiding its followers. They succeeded in

---

[11] al-Kulaynī, *al-Kāfī*, 2:636.

[12] al-ʿĀmilī, *Wasāʾil al-shīʿah*, 12:143.

creating a corps of scholars within a strong and independent community of Muslims. Through this achievement, they were able to preserve a wealth of knowledge and heritage.

How did they do this? It was not through making uncalculated emotional stances. It was not by acting on the moment or for the moment. They had a true long-term vision for their followers. We see this, for example, in the stance of Imam al-Ḥasan and his decision to strike a truce with Muʿāwiyah. Despite the assassination attempts and despite being ridiculed by people near and far,[13] he did not allow anything to cloud his judgement. He could have easily led his followers into a losing battle and become a martyr. Yet the time had not come for that. Muʿāwiyah was not like Yazīd. Imam al-Ḥasan's martyrdom would not have reaped the same fruits as Imam al-Ḥusayn's. More of this can be read in the books dedicated to studying this movement. The conclusion that we wish to draw here is the incredible focus that the Holy Household had on preserving their followers and their teachings – not only in the short term, but over the centuries to come.

The Messenger and the Guardian

The Holy Prophet came with a complete message that he delivered during his lifetime. Many of the details had still to be given and so divine providence decreed that he give the detailed message and the task of elucidating and applying its details to his cousin and viceroy ʿAlī ibn Abī Ṭālib, who would then in turn apply that message, delivering its details and explanation to the people.

The knowledge that the Holy Prophet gave to Imam ʿAlī was not like any other typical knowledge. It was of the special quality and quantity that we have discussed before. Imam ʿAlī says,

علّمني رسول الله (ص) ألف باب يفتح كلّ باب ألف باب

The Messenger of God taught me a thousand gates [of knowledge] and each gate opens a thousand more.[14]

If we understand Imam ʿAlī's succession to the Holy Prophet in this light, we will understand some of the words of the Holy Household speaking of their knowledge. Imam al-Bāqir would say,

---

[13] See: Chamseddine, *Hussain's Revolution*, 117-25.

[14] al-Majlisī, *Biḥār al-anwār*, 26:29.

ليس عند أحد من الناس حق ولا صواب ولا أحد من الناس يقضي بقضاء حق إلا ما خرج منا أهل البيت وإذا تشعبت بهم الأمور كان الخطاء منهم والصواب من علي عليه السلام.

No individual possesses any truth or correct [understanding], nor is there any individual that administers a just judgement, except what comes from us Ahl al-Bayt. If matters confounded them, any mistake was from them and any correct action was from ʿAlī.[15]

Upon reflection, we find this conclusion to be completely rational, especially in light of the close connection between the Holy Prophet and Imam ʿAlī. Considering historical realities, it would not make sense to claim that anyone had more knowledge of the message than the Holy Household. As Imam al-Ṣādiq explains,

عجبا للناس إنهم اخذوا علمهم كله عن رسول الله صلى الله عليه وآله، فعملوا به واهتدوا ويرون أن أهل بيته لم يأخذوا علمه، ونحن أهل بيته وذريته في منازلنا نزل الوحي، ومن عندنا خرج العلم إليهم، أفيرون أنهم علموا واهتدوا وجهلنا نحن وضللنا، إن هذا لمحال.

I marvel at people who [claim to] have taken all their knowledge from the Messenger of God and have applied it and were guided by it, yet they believe that the people of his household did not take his knowledge! We are the people of his household and his progeny. In our houses the revelations descended and from us knowledge emanated to them! So, do they believe that they know and were guided, while we are ignorant and misguided? That is surely an impossibility! [16]

Our understanding is that the entirety of the message was delivered to the people during the lifetime of the Holy Prophet. This is understood from a number of holy verses and noble traditions. For example, we know that the Holy Qurʾan was delivered in its entirety during the lifetime of the Holy Prophet. By its own words, the Holy Qurʾan is a 'clarification of all things.'

وَنَزَّلْنَا عَلَيْكَ الْكِتَابَ تِبْيَانًا لِّكُلِّ شَيْءٍ وَهُدًى وَرَحْمَةً وَبُشْرَىٰ لِلْمُسْلِمِينَ

We have sent down the Book to you as a clarification of all things and as guidance, mercy and good news for the Muslims.[17]

---

[15] al-Kulaynī, *al-Kāfī*, 1:399.

[16] Ibid, 1:398.

[17] The Holy Qurʾan, 16:89.

How do we reconcile the fact that the Holy Prophet delivered a complete message with the idea that his progeny held religious knowledge that others did not? The two ideas are not contradictory, especially when keeping in mind that the Holy Qur'an provides a general framework while the narrations fill in the details. Narrations simply bring to the forefront some details present within the Holy Qur'an but which we cannot independently draw out. That is why the imams of the Holy Household would tell their followers to ask them from where in the Holy Qur'an they drew each idea, and they will show them. For example, Imam al-Bāqir would say,

إذا حدثتكم بشيء فاسألوني من كتاب الله

> *If I speak to you about any matter, ask me [*to *for its support] from the Book of God.*[18]

Neither is the interplay between the Holy Qur'an and the noble traditions an implausible, nor even an uncommon, phenomenon. We can draw numerous examples of similar relationships between general frameworks and detailed knowledge.

For example, how would we apply instructions to 'respect every scholar'? How do we know that any given individual is a scholar? According to Oxford Dictionary, a scholar is "a specialist in a particular branch of study." We need to know who has specialized expertise in order to adequately apply the general instructive statement. We may gain this knowledge from personal first-hand experience. It may be such a widely known fact that its truth has become a given. It may be through the testimony of other experts. The fact that we may not know who is and who is not a scholar does not take away from the completeness of the instructions we started with.

Another example can be seen in the legal systems of many contemporary governments. Each has its constitution and its bureaucracy. But a bureaucrat sitting in his office does not directly apply the constitution. The legislature must first enact laws drawn out of the constitution's general provisions. The executive fills in the details of how those laws are applied. A court or two may weigh in on how these applications square up against the state's constitution. These additional layers do not mean

---

[18] al-Kulaynī, *al-Kāfī*, 1:60.

that the constitution is deficient in any way. They only fill in the details within the general outlines laid out by that primary document.

The same applies to the Holy Qur'an. It contains a complete and holistic message, but one that is not expressed in minute details within the covers of a single book. The infallible interpretation and application of all of its guidelines require the immaculate Imam.

Accepting the elucidations and interpretations of the Holy Qur'an that came to us through the household of the Prophet created a distinct scholastic history and heritage for their followers. On the other hand, those who declined to follow the Holy Household were pressed to follow their own speculative opinions. They produced ideas such as *al-ra'y*, *qiyās*, and *istiṣlāḥ* in order to arrive at religious rulings where not enough evidence can be found. As such, their reasoned deduction – *ijtihād* – was parallel to the naṣṣ instead of being subservient to it.

The great wealth of knowledge that the Holy Household left their followers ensured that their followers do not face that problem. The elucidation and explanations of the imams provide enough guidance on the meaning of the Holy Qur'an. Thus, for the followers of the Holy Household, *ijtihād* became subordinate to explicit and clear text (naṣṣ). Every religious ruling must ultimately have some basis in naṣṣ.

When we contemplate the words of the Holy Household, we see that their explanations bring out the subtle, hidden meanings of Holy Qur'an. Yet these subtle meanings are always based upon an explicit common sense understanding of the scripture. Their elucidations are never contradictory, or even counterintuitive, to a learned reading of the religious evidence. We should reflect on these points with some intellectual humility.

The difference in religious heritage and its implications on the concept of *ijtihād* are profound. Numerous narrations lay out the criteria for valid *ijtihād* in the school of the Holy Household. The result is a process of rational deduction that revolves around understanding the scriptural text rather than supplementing it. In both instances, reason is used to arrive at conclusions that may or may not be correct. However, we commit a grave mistake when reason is not made subordinate to the divine scripture but a supplemental source of legislation. This means that we allow our own intellects, with its preconceptions and influences, to legislate.

This is why when ʿAllāmah Ṭabāṭabāʾī speaks of Hadith al-Thaqalayn, he says that to abandon one of the two weighty things is to abandon both.[19]

The Guardian's Legacy

We thus come to understand religious authority as the product of some particular knowledge, of special quantity and quality, which the rightful imams possess. In this way, it is very similar to political authority as we have come to understand it through the previous discussions.

In fact, if we are left with just one narration – that the Holy Prophet had taught Imam ʿAlī "a thousand gates [of knowledge] and each gate opens a thousand more" – that would be enough for us to believe in Imam ʿAlī's religious authority. Even if we put aside all the narrations about how the Holy Prophet taught Imam ʿAlī the detailed meanings of the Holy Qurʾan, that one narration would suffice us. Who else can claim to have gained such knowledge from the Messenger of God?

Yet when we look at history, we witness the great intellectual crimes committed against the Holy Household. If we simply look at the founders of the four *madhāhib* of Sunni Islam, we find that they were all either students of Imam al-Ṣādiq or students of his students. Imam al-Bāqir would narrate directly quoting the Holy Prophet without mentioning from whom he heard it. Everyone would accept his narrations because they knew he was relaying from his father and grandfathers all the way back to the Holy Prophet.

When Imam al-Bāqir passed away, Sālim ibn Abū Ḥafṣah went to condole his son Imam al-Ṣādiq. In condoling the Imam, Sālim said,

> *Surely, we are of God and surely to Him we shall return. An individual the like of* whom *we have not seen has departed us. He used to say 'the Messenger of God said' and would not be asked about who relayed those traditions from the Messenger of God to him.*[20]

The tragedy lies in the fact that we scarcely find any narrations from our Imams in the books of these students that went on to become the leaders of the other schools of thought. Why? There was a great deal of political pressure to exclude the Holy Household from any public discourse. The

---

[19] al-Ṭabāṭabāʾī, *al-Mīzān*, exegesis of verses 5:15-19.

[20] al-Ṭūsī, *al-Amālī*, 125.

powers at the time knew that hearts and minds always gravitated to the progeny of the Holy Prophet. They knew that if the imams were allowed to freely exercise religious leadership, they would have the devotion of the entire Muslim ummah. The rulers would no longer be free to act as they liked so long as the Holy Household had its say. In fact, political authority could shift to the Holy Household if it gains that kind of devotion. The political authorities of the time thus strived to keep the Holy Household out of public view and away from any public discourse.

Muslim rulers attempted to usurp religious authority along with political authority. Unfortunately, the farce did fool some of the public scholars of the time. We simply wonder, if political power can be usurped by force, can knowledge and religious authority be usurped in the same way? Force cannot make the governor a doctor or astronomer. Nor can it make him an expert in the Holy Qur'an and noble traditions.

That is why it was so critical for the Holy Prophet to appoint a successor after him, especially as a religious authority that would continue to guide the Muslim ummah. Imam al-Ṣādiq relays the following conversation between his father and one of his companions:

> إلى أن قال: وإن كان رسول الله (ص) لم يستخلف أحداً فقد ضيّع مَن في أصلاب الرجال ممّن يكون بعده، قال: وما يكفيهم القرآن؟ قال: بلى لو وجدوا له مفسّراً ، قال: وما فسّره رسول الله (ص)؟ قال: بلى قد فسّره لرجل واحد، وفسّر للأمّة شأن ذلك الرجل، وهو عليّ بن أبي طالب (ع)
>
> *[My father said,] 'And if the Messenger of God did not appoint anyone as successor, then he surely would have been forsaking those who are in the loins of men who would come after him.' He [the narrator] said, 'Would the Qur'an not suffice them?' [Imam al-Bāqir] said, 'Yes, if only they could find someone to interpret it.' He asked, 'Did the Messenger of God not interpret it?' [Imam al-Bāqir] said, 'Yes he did, but to a single individual and explained to the ummah the status of that man. That man was ʿAlī ibn Abī Ṭālib.'*[21]

Recap

Before moving on to our next topic, let us reflect on the understanding we have reached of immaculacy and its significance.

---

[21] al-ʿĀmilī, *Wasāʾil al-shīʿah*, 27:178.

First, immaculacy provides its holder with the qualifications for religious and temporal authority. As we have discussed, immaculacy is derived from a particular knowledge that is certain and immutable. Possessing that knowledge gives the individual the highest of qualifications, making them the ideal candidates for positions of authority.

Second, immaculacy means that any exercise of religious or temporal authority outside the purview of the immaculate is a rational mistake. From the religious perspective, it is clear that acting against the words of an immaculate imam would be an error. Immaculacy dictates that such action is not only a religious mistake, but a rational error as well. If you know something is certain and immutable, how can you act contrary to it without falling into an intellectual contradiction? Thus, when the immaculate or his immaculate teachings are accessible, the exercise of religious authority outside those teachings and dictates is based on erroneous epistemological foundations. Similarly, the exercise of any temporal authority in the presence of an immaculate, without his approval, is a usurpation of that position and an exercise of illegitimate force.

Third, knowing that immaculacy is a trait gained and maintained by the individual's free will and choice, we understand the great deal of effort required to maintain it. We cannot compare their perseverance and worship to ours. Theirs is based on a particular knowledge which they must go through great lengths to maintain. That is why those possessing the trait of immaculacy are the ones that face the greatest trials and tribulations. When asked who faces the greatest tests, the noble traditions answer,

النبيون ثم الأمثل فالأمثل

> *The prophets, then those of the greatest excellence and the next greatest [and so forth].*[22]

From this, we understand the words of the Holy Prophet Muḥammad in describing the trials he faced in this world.

ما أوذي نبي مثل ما أوذيت

> *No prophet has been hurt to the degree that I have been hurt.*[23]

Perseverance in the face of tests and hardships is integral to their merit. Because of this, we find them to be the humblest of individuals, despite

---

[22] al-Kulaynī, *al-Kāfī*, 2:252.

[23] al-Majlisī, *Biḥār al-anwār*, 39:56.

having the greatest qualities and qualifications. Even though they are ones with the most rightful claim to authority, we find that they do not cling to the prestige of chiefs and kings.

We must also be aware of the correlation between knowledge and good work. Many noble traditions point out that those with greater knowledge are held to a higher standard of conduct. A person that 'does not know any better' may be excused for his ignorance. But scholars and intellectuals are held to a higher standard because of their higher awareness. The highest of standards are held for those who possess this particular knowledge, where nothing short of immaculate character is expected.

Some ask, 'If these individuals were immaculate, why do we find them to be always fearful of God and asking for His forgiveness?' The answer lies in this understanding of where immaculacy originates and how it is maintained. Immaculacy is not a free ticket to paradise. It is an error to think of immaculacy simply as freedom from error. We must understand that it is attained and maintained through the individual's free choice. We must contemplate its relationship to knowledge, perseverance, and worship. It is their excellence in perseverance, devotion, character, and conduct made them recipients of God's wisely bestowed grace, protection, and immaculacy – allowing them to be the greatest role models that humanity can hope for.

PART II
PRACTICAL IMPLICATIONS

ON NAṢṢ

FIVE MEANINGS OF NAṢṢ

Our respected scholars often state that the succession of Imam ʿAlī to the Holy Prophet is supported by *naṣṣ* or *dalīl naṣṣī*.[1] What exactly does that mean?

There are multiple technical usages to this word within the realm of Islamic sciences.

First, the word naṣṣ is used to refer to divine legislation. It denotes religious evidence as opposed to personal opinions, political considerations, or anything of the like. Our scholars say that the followers of the Holy Household rely on naṣṣ in the process of *ijtihād*. The connotation is that *ijtihād* is limited to interpretation of the religious evidentiary record. All other tools – such as reason and experience – are at the service of the Holy Qur'an and noble traditions, and not parallel to them. The aim of *ijtihād* is to gain the best understanding of the text that we can arrive to.

Second, our scholars may refer to naṣṣ as opposed to *ẓāhir*. Here, *dalīl naṣṣī* is used to indicate the existence of absolute and immutable evidence in support of a certain conclusion. For example, we may say that

---

1 *Naṣṣ* (past tense verb): raised, demonstrated. al-Anṣārī says, "And amongst its meanings are *naṣṣ al-Qur'an* and *naṣṣ al-ḥadīth*, meaning the rules signified by their apparent meanings." See: *Lisān al-ʿarab, s.v.* N-Ṣ-Ṣ (*nūn-ṣād-ṣād*). *Naṣṣ* can properly be understood as "divine declaration." The word is so broad that it has been used to denote a multitude of meanings in technical writings.

a Muslim's obligation to pray five times a day is supported by naṣṣ. The evidence in this regard is so great and explicit, that no Muslim doubts that statement. On the other hand, our scholars rely on the *ẓāhir* – or apparent – meaning when interpreting Qur'anic verses and noble traditions. The apparent meanings of religious texts provide strong evidence for the interpreting scholar. However, the possibility remains that the apparent meaning may be contradicted if and when strong evidence to the contrary can be found.

Third, naṣṣ may be used to indicate the exact transmission of a pronouncement, as opposed to transmission of its meanings. When we refer to *naṣṣ al-hadīth*, we are speaking of its text and not its meaning, implications, connotations, etc.

Fourth, our scholars refer to naṣṣ as *dalīl lafẓī* as opposed to *dalīl lubbī* – direct uttered evidence as opposed to analytical evidence. There is naṣṣ in support of a certain religious ruling if there is a Qur'anic verse or noble tradition that addresses the issue.[2] However, there may be evidence that is not based on a direct statement of the Holy Qur'an, the Holy Prophet, or the Immaculate Imams. Such evidence may come from rational norm (*al-sīrah al-'uqalā'iyyah*), the judgment of practical and theoretical reason, the unanimity of scholars, and religious necessity.[3]

For example, if Muslims at the time of the Holy Prophet engaged in a given activity and the Holy Prophet did not encourage it or admonish them against it in any way, then we can conclude that the action in question is permissible. Our conclusion did not depend on a specific declaration, but on the Holy Prophet's tacit approval. Thus, we would say that there is *dalīl lubbī* here but no *dalīl lafẓī*.

Take again the example of engaging in trade and business. People before and during the time of the Holy Prophet and the Immaculate Imams engaged in trade and entered into contracts. Engaging in labor, trade, and contracts is just a part of rational norm – one type of analytical evidence. The Holy Household's explicit approval of their actions is a form of direct evidence in support of trade's permissibility. The numerous

---

[2] Naṣṣ as direct evidence does not only include the spoken and written words of the Holy Qur'an and noble traditions, but also includes other implicit evidence. For example, the context in which a verse was revealed is an important part of the evidentiary record.

[3] These listed concepts are well known to a student of *uṣūl al-fiqh*. The reader can find detailed expositions of these and other concepts addressed in this chapter through study of seminary textbooks on the topic.

instances where the Holy Qur'an and the Holy Household verbally encouraged people to engage in trade and business are naṣṣ in support of that ruling.

As the reader can see, there are some instances where both *dalīl naṣṣī* and *dalīl lubbī* are present. The existence of *dalīl lubbī* does not preclude the existence of *dalīl naṣṣī* on the subject. For example, a ruling may be supported by explicit verses and traditions, as well as tacit approvals, scholarly unanimity, and the judgement of practical reason.

Al-dalīl al-naṣṣī as direct evidence can be categorize into three types:

- *Dalīl imḍā'ī* (validating evidence) that supports and corroborates a *dalīl lubbī*. It shows that naṣṣ (revelation) and *lubb* (reason) are consistent. In this case, *al-dalīl al-naṣṣī* is not the starting point but comes on the backdrop of analytical evidence that existed before it.
- *Dalīl irshādī* (instructive evidence) that guides us towards a *dalīl lubbī*. Again, *al-dalīl al-naṣṣī* is not the starting point in these instances but comes to direct our attention to previously existing analytical evidence.[4]
- *Dalīl ta'sīsī* (foundational evidence) which is not preceded by any analytical evidence. It is thus *dalīl ta'abbudī* (devotional evidence) which we accept as a matter of faith, whether or not we know the prudential aim (*milāk*) behind it.

Al-dalīl al-ta'sīsī can also be divided into three categories:

- Pure *ta'sīsī* evidence, with no indication of the prudential aim behind it. This type is purely devotional and includes many of the rules outlined in the books of jurisprudence.
- *Ta'sīsī* evidence that is accompanied by a partial explanation of the prudential aim behind it. For example, the Holy Qur'an does not only call us to prayer, but informs us that it 'restrains from indecent and wrongful conduct.'[5] A jurist can sometimes rely on these partially explained prudential aims in their deductions of religious laws.

---

[4] Note that the usefulness of *al-dalīl al-imḍa'ī* and *al-dalīl al-irshādī* is not limited to verification and instruction. Rather, direct evidence has scope, context, and other indications that are not present in *al-dalīl al-lubbi*, making *al-dalīl al-naṣṣi* generally more useful.

[5] The Holy Qur'an, 29:45.

- *Taʾsīsī* evidence that is accompanied by a full explanation of the prudential aim behind it. This type of evidence does not exist, as the wisdom behind divine laws are not fully attainable to our minds. As such, we are not obligated to know or seek them. Religious laws are not deduced based on a jurist's understanding of divine wisdom. Rather, they are deduced based on evidence that addresses diverse subjects. The role of the jurist is to deduce the rule regarding each subject, regardless of the prudential aim behind it.

Take the obligation of fasting as an example. There are plenty of narrations stating different aims and reasons for why fasting was made obligatory. It is a means for us to remember the hunger and thirst of the poor, as well as to contemplate the hunger and thirst of the Day of Judgement. It is a means of purifying our body and our spirits. It is a training season to fortify ourselves for the challenges of the coming year. However, we do not use this knowledge to alter the religious rulings in any way.

Even when the prudential aims (*milākāt* or *maqāṣid*) of a ruling seem clear, our scholars will abide by the naṣṣ in order not to allow their personal opinions to affect the conclusion. Take the example of the mandatory waiting period (*ʿiddah*) that a divorced or widowed woman must go through before remarrying. The prudential aim of that rule seems clear – to ensure that she is not pregnant. However, now that we have the technology to determine whether a woman is pregnant or not in a shorter period, do we undo the waiting period that the naṣṣ mandates? Our scholars agree that the answer is no. Our school of thought does not rely on individual opinions and preferences. Though the prudential aim of the rule might seem clear at first glance, who are we to say that it was God's only aim in instituting this rule? To assume that we can comprehensively understand the purposes behind God's legislation would be to substitute His infinite wisdom with our limited vision. This is a clear error that the scholars from this school of thought avoid.

Fifth, naṣṣ can be used to indicate divine declaration and establishment. For example, we may say that a certain subject is *manṣūṣ*, indicating that it is proclaimed by a higher authority.

The reader should note that these five meanings of naṣṣ are not mutually exclusive. *Naṣṣ* may be used for more than one of these meanings in any specific instance, depending on the varied angles and facets of the subject.

For example, we can say that there is naṣṣ in support of the obligation of prayer. This means:

1. there is religious evidence, not mere personal opinions and considerations;
2. there is clear and immutable evidence, and we are not merely relying on the apparent meaning of a verse or tradition;
3. the evidence was transmitted exactly, not by summary or meaning;
4. there is direct evidence that goes beyond *al-dalīl al-lubbī*; and
5. the evidence is foundational (*taʾsīsī*) and not only validating (*imḍaʾī*) or instructive (*irshādī*).

Naṣṣ as Divine Declaration

The Shia have so greatly emphasized the idea of naṣṣ that it has become a integral part of their theological framework, especially of imamate. But which of the above meanings of naṣṣ do they denote when using this word?

Principally, naṣṣ is used in reference to imamate to indicate the fifth meaning presented above – divine declaration and establishment. That is, Shia doctrine dictates that the position of imamate cannot be reached without the title being divinely bestowed.

Note that the theoretical proofs for the necessity of imamate do not dictate that there must be any naṣṣ in the fourth meaning. In other words, there is no evidence that a *dalīl lafẓī* is required in establishing imamate. The evidence can (theoretically speaking) be entirely *lubbī*.

This is not to say that the *dalīl lafẓī* in this regard is lacking. On the contrary, the direct evidence – Qurʾanic verses and prophetic traditions – is so overwhelming as to leave no room for doubt.

However, this means that the direct evidence is not foundational (*taʾsīsī*) on the subject. It is instructive (*irshādī*) in that it guides us toward a conclusion that can theoretically be reached through exercising reason alone.

The Alternatives to Naṣṣ

We can see from the foregoing that the position that naṣṣ is required on the issue of imamate means that legitimacy in this regard can only be derived from a divine source. We have also established previously that imamate is a human necessity, with the imam taking the role of humanity's collective practical reason.

There are four questions that have historically been central to the discussion of naṣṣ and legitimacy. Must a ruler abide by the rule of law, or are they above the law? What are the qualifications that allow a ruler to assume that position? How does the ummah's choice relate to legitimacy? Does the fact that an individual is in a position authority grant them any special privileges or legitimacy?

The principle of naṣṣ allows us to eliminate the following three alternatives.

First, that God delegated the matter of selecting an imam to the people and their choice. The ummah's choice is given importance in installing a ruler, but not thereafter. Some theories place the power of choice in an oligarchic *shūrā*, or council, of the elites. Other theories place importance on the consensus of the people of Medina. The bottom line in these theories is that the caliph assumes that position only with the blessings of the ummah. But what happens if the individual does not abide by Islam's laws? What if the individual is corrupt and abusive? These considerations are immaterial so long as the individual was initially met with the ummah's approval.

Second, the Ashāʿirah[6] make an argument based on the legitimacy of what transpired; the fact that certain individuals became caliphs means that they had legitimacy. This alternative suggests that there are no qualifications for the individual who fills the position of caliph. Thus, whoever becomes caliph takes legitimacy from their filling of the position. There is no law or rule that would make one caliph acceptable and another not.

This is similar to the *Ashʿarī* belief in regard to God's actions. A major tenet of their school is a belief that good and evil are not objective realities. Rather, whatever God does is good, and whatever He forbids is evil; God determines exclusively and arbitrarily the value of actions.[7]

---

[6] This is not simply a Sunni Ashʿarī argument, but is more widespread about Sunni traditionalist. Classical Ashʿarī arguments tend to reject naṣṣ (and indeed the multiple corroborating narrations such as Ghadīr Khumm) for any specific successor to the Prophet. Instead, they affirm that the consensus and authority of the community was such to accept what happened. See: al-Juwaynī, *A Guide to Conclusive Proofs*, 225–35.

[7] This is known as divine command ethics. See: al-Attar, *Islamic Ethics*.

This is why historically we find that claims of legitimacy transformed with circumstances. Some caliphs claimed that title based on *shūrā*. Others came through the appointment of the prior caliph. Still others came though the selection of a council appointed by the previous caliph.

Imam ʿAlī was burdened with political leadership when the Muslim community paid allegiance to him. Then came Muʿāwiyah who claimed rule through the sword and installed a monarchical system for his family.

Which of these methods of claiming political power was legitimate? The Muslim ummah, with the exception of a small opposition, seemed to believe that all of these were legitimate claims to power with no real philosophical or ideological explanation. To them, legitimacy laid in the hands of the victor. They continued to deal with the ruler as the successor of the Holy Prophet. They issued verdicts prohibiting any dissent or rebellion against the ruling power.

The Holy Household and their followers were the major opposition in those periods. They were the voice that called for an honest assessment of reality and the return to a proper standard by which to evaluate the rulers. They called for naṣṣ to be the arbiter of who can claim legitimacy. In their eyes, the sole source of legitimacy was explicit religious evidence in support of any claim to successorship to the Holy Prophet.

The Ashʿarī theory of legitimacy did not place any importance on whether the ruler abided by the law or was corrupt. What is important is that they were the ruler. Neither was the ummah's will and choice given any importance. So long as a ruler was at the helm, he carried legitimacy and the ummah ought to follow him.

Both of these alternatives are contrary to the idea of imamate as a divinely dictated and legitimized position in succession to the Holy Prophet. Accepting such divine dictates leads to the principle of abiding by naṣṣ and everything that it entails. This theory has put much emphasis on the ruler's duty to abide by Islam's laws – to the degree that the individual must be immaculate. It also put great emphasis on the exceptional characteristics of an imam, including their particular knowledge, passing of arduous trials, and the like.

Accepting the necessity of naṣṣ means that the ummah has no authority to confer legitimacy to whomever it wishes (or whomever fills the position). Legitimacy is derived from the heavens, not from the masses. However, this does not mean that an imam imposes his authority on the ummah even if it rejects him. It is the role and duty of the ummah to empower the imam and allow him the space to fully exercise his divinely endowed authority.

If the ummah abandons and rejects the imam, it is to its own detriment and misfortune. The imam will not impose his authority by force. This is what happened historically, for example, when the ummah rejected the Commander of the Faithful for about two decades before they swore allegiance to him en masse. He did not seek to impose his authority during that time but did so when the ummah chose to allow him the exercise of his authority.

Third, the principle of naṣṣ also allows us to eliminate the alternative of human political institutions. In human non-religious thought, philosophies have emerged that solve some of the first two alternative's subproblems. Modern political philosophies put legitimacy in the hands of the people, rejecting the rule of oppression and abuse. They establish qualifications for a leader such as experience and integrity. They write and promulgate constitutions and forbid a leader from controverting or subverting it, or else they would be removed from office.

This third alternative is also contrary to the principle of naṣṣ. Naṣṣ dictates that legitimacy is drawn from the divine, whereas modern political philosophies draw legitimacy from the citizenry, from the sovereignty of the people. In modern political philosophies, religion may be a source of legislation. It is the sole source of legislation for leadership established by naṣṣ. In modern political philosophies, the qualifications of a leader are few and diluted, such as integrity and experience. The leadership of naṣṣ allows nothing short of immaculacy.[8]

---

[8] The subject of this book is immaculate imamate as a foundational religious belief, alongside tawḥīd, nubuwwah, and the Day of Resurrection. This book addresses the concept of imamate as the position of guidance and succession to the Holy Prophet. The principle of naṣṣ states that imamate is connected to divine authority and dictates. But what happens when the individual who is appointed as imam by the heavens is absent or inaccessible (as is the case during the time of *ghaybah*)? Naṣṣ provides legitimacy and authority for the divinely appointed imam – whether present or absent, accessible or inaccessible. We mentioned that the role of the ummah toward an imam is to empower him (in his presence) and allow him the space to fully exercise his divinely endowed authority. During the time of *ghaybah*, the ummah's role is *intiẓār al-faraj* (awaiting relief) as dictated in countless traditions.

As for the ummah's political stance during the time of *ghaybah*, that is outside the scope of the principle of imamate, and thus outside the scope of this book. Jurists have disagreed on this issue – from the far-right opinion of *wilāyat al-faqīh* (authority of the jurist) and the call for a religious government, to the far-left opinion of *wilāyat al-ummah ʿalā*

Naṣṣ dictates that legitimacy is not acquired through force or heredity. It is not acquired by fiat or through a ballot box. Naṣṣ dictates that legitimacy is acquired solely through divine appointment.

NECESSITY OF NAṢṢ

One group of Muslims said that naṣṣ existed in naming a successor to the Holy Prophet. This group's claimed became a center of debate. Their opponents said that there was no naṣṣ, and that the cited proofs were lacking in evidentiary quality. They stated that some noble traditions cited were not admissible as evidence because they lacked the proper chain of narrators, and therefore their truth could be ascertained. When they could not reject a source's validity, the claim was that it did not conclusively convey the meaning for which it was asserted.

Analyzing this debate, we can draw an important conclusion – that naṣṣ, if it exists, holds supremacy over all other methods by which a caliph could claim title. If this were not the case, the debate would not have centered around whether the naṣṣ is useful to prove successorship. The assertion would have been that the council's decision supersedes the naṣṣ, or that the appointment of the previous caliph is equal to the naṣṣ, or that the claim of force renders the naṣṣ moot. None of these assertions were made. Instead, the debate centered around how genuine and probative the naṣṣ might be.

The Holy Household and their followers made an assertion about naṣṣ that went a step further. They stated that not only did the naṣṣ exist, but that its existence was a matter of rational and theological necessity. Just as a prophet needs a miracle to prove his prophethood, an imam – in the comprehensive sense that we have outlined earlier, not merely an administrative or scholarly figure – must have naṣṣ to support his succession and guardianship. Only God would know who is immaculate material, knowing whatever they express or bury deep in their hearts.

Why do prophets need miracles? Because their claim is that they have a connection to something beyond this physical world. God's grace dictates that He provides the means by which this claim can be conclusively verified. If the prophets' preaching was based solely on human reasoning, there is only so far that their rational arguments could go. Sure, this

---

nafsihā (authority of the ummah over itself) and the call for civil authority. This is a jurisprudential subject distinct from the topic of imamate, which may be addressed in a future book – if God grants the opportunity.

wise person makes a plausible claim about a world beyond our senses. But how are we to know for sure that they are speaking on behalf of God? Is there a sign of their connection to that world beyond? A miracle is needed in order to prove their connection. Otherwise, they will be seen as philosophers with no greater connection to the truth than anyone else. Thus, in order to prove their connection to the unseen without a doubt, they rely on miracles that go beyond the natural.[9]

Our school of thought's emphasis on the necessity of naṣṣ is based on its understanding of imamate and on historical fact according to generations of trusted followers of the Holy Household. Because we believe imamate to be more than just temporal leadership, we believe that it requires more than just temporal sources of legitimacy. Because imamate is an authority that stems from a particular knowledge, we must have evidence that the individual is privy to that particular knowledge. That is not something that any of us can assess with our limited faculties and resources. Thus, there needs to be some form of evidence that gives us certainty about the individual's merits and position. Prophet Muḥammad's word testifying to the person's qualifications suffices to provide this assurance.

Therefore, having understood imamate as that position of merit that comes through particular knowledge, distinguished works, and unmatched perseverance, are we able to identify which individual has these traits? We cannot conclude that any particular individual holds the status of imamate through our limited observations and analyses. God Almighty would not appoint for us an imam and expect us to follow him without providing us with the proper tools to know who he is. Therefore, God would have – out of his boundless grace and mercy – provided us with the necessary evidence to know that person. Having sent His Messenger with a holy scripture and divine message, He would have instructed that the Holy Prophet inform the people about their imam. Thus, naṣṣ must exist indicating the identity of the imam and successor after the Holy Prophet.[10]

---

[9] For a discussion of this point, see: al-Ḥillī, *Kashf al-murād*, 474–75.

[10] See: al-Ḥillī, *Kashf al-murād*, 495–96.

BETWEEN NAṢṢ AND REASON

In every science, the researcher studies and assesses all available and possible proofs for any given statement. The same is true for the Islamic sciences such as fiqh, uṣūl, and kalām. A Muslim researcher begins with the Holy Qur'an and noble traditions, and continues down the chain of evidence to assess the validity of scholastic unanimity and prevailing opinions. These evidentiary sources are not all at the same level. Rather, some are of a higher order than others. Still, researchers do not suffice themselves with studying the highest order of evidence. They go down the hierarchy and discuss every piece of evidence at every level.

For example, there are books written on immaculacy that take a comprehensive view of the evidence – from Qur'anic verses, to noble traditions, to rational discussions, etc. There are other books that are solely aimed at studying the Qur'anic verses that superficially seem contrary to immaculacy. The authors of such books take immaculacy as a given. However, that did not stop them from taken the verses one by one and addressing any apparent contradiction – thus clearing and strengthening the evidentiary record in support of the idea.

The point is that scholars take a comprehensive look at the evidence and provide a plethora of proofs in support of their claims. Why do they do so even though a single argument or proof may be enough to establish a statement's truth?

First, a holistic view of the evidence provides a 'fail-safe' system of beliefs. If a piece of evidence comes into question, or if the epistemic framework of the researcher changes to exclude a piece of evidence, then there remains a plethora of proofs that one can still rely on. A holistic view allows for a more stable and enduring belief system.

Second, doubt, knowledge, and certainty come in grades. Amassing evidence allows the individual to move from doubt to confidence and from confidence. Amassing evidence allows an individual to strengthen their confidence in a statement, up to the point of certainty.

Taking a comprehensive and holistic view of the evidence is not an exercise in intellectual luxury or sport. Rather, the process leads to a higher quality of knowledge and belief, rooted in thoroughly vetted evidence.

Third, when engaging in dialogue with others, it is best to start at a point of shared understanding. Having a plethora of evidence and proof allows for many points of shared understanding that can be used in dialogue.

TWO FACETS OF IMAMATE

There are two facets of imamate, each supported with a range of evidence.

First, we believe that imamate is a position that draws its legitimacy from God's authority. Naṣṣ, as divine declaration evidenced by conclusive direct uttered evidence (*dalīl lafẓī qaṭʿī*), informs us of God's authoritative act of appointing an imam. There is no alternative to naṣṣ as evidence in this regard.

Second, we believe that imamate has a set of conditions based on the reality, necessity, duties, and qualifications for the position. This facet is analytical and is tied not to divine authority but to practical reason. Evidence of this facet is not limited to naṣṣ. The range of evidence that can be used in this regard extends beyond naṣṣ to include other forms.

The question becomes, is the naṣṣ that appoints an imam pure *dalīl taʾsīsī* (foundational evidence) that does not provide the prudential reasons behind its content? Must we accept it as a matter of faith and devotion (*taʿabbud*), without knowing the prudential aim (*milāk*) behind it? Or is it instructive and validating evidence, such that the naṣṣ on the subject is helpful but not indispensable?

Is the naṣṣ purely foundational, asking us to follow its directives out of devotion alone? Or is it instructive and validating, providing the basis and context of those directives?

A perusal of the noble traditions that appointed an imam or spoke of his character will yield a clear answer. The traditions do not ask us to follow the imam out of devotion only. They guide us to the imam's qualities and qualifications in terms clearly understood by any reasonable individual. They coupled the appointment by a characterization that the imam is the 'most knowledgeable,' 'most pious,' 'most judicious,' 'bravest,' etc.

Does Naṣṣ Limit Reason?

Does naṣṣ limit the role of reason in identifying and following an imam? Let us take a quick look at prophethood before we answer these question about imamate.

How can we ascertain the truth of an individual's claim to prophethood? As we mentioned, a prophet would be able to use a miracle as clear demonstrative evidence of his connection to a higher realm. But is there an alternative to miracles? Is there a rational way to determine the truth of such a claim?

We find that the Holy Prophet Muḥammad provided an answer to that early on in his preaching of the message. The Holy Qur᾽an was revealed verse by verse, so many Muslims at the time did not have the opportunity to comprehensively analyze the book. However, many believed in the truth of the Holy Prophet's message because of the grandeur and excellence of his character. Even before he began preaching, he was known as honest and trustworthy. Having been the most truthful and trustworthy, exhibiting immaculate character for forty years, he earned a chance at being heard and believed. Yes, this may not have been enough for many people, especially considering the gravity of the claim. For them, a miracle was necessary as a general and evident proof. However, all this is to say that a miracle is not the exclusive means by which we can judge the truth of a claim to prophethood.

This same concept can be applied to imamate. While naṣṣ is the general and evident proof in assessing an individual's claim to imamate, it is not the exclusive means at our disposal. The fact that naṣṣ exists does not mean that our rational processes should be ignored and that the issue of imamate is left without any other known standards or criteria.

If we assume, for the sake of argument, that there was no naṣṣ appointing Imam ʿAlī as the successor of the Holy Prophet, can we use reason to conclude that he was in fact the rightful successor – an imam in the sense we have so far described?

Definitely. We simply need to go back to the plentiful praise and many merits mentioned in the books of history about this magnificent personality. Those are enough for us to reasonably conclude that he is most qualified – if not the only qualified individual – to succeed the Holy Prophet.

When the event of Ghadīr Khumm is mentioned, those outside our school of thought attempt to cast doubt on its significance. Some will doubt its authenticity, denying the overwhelming evidence of its truth. Others will say that the Holy Prophet simply wanted to showcase his affection to Imam ʿAlī and not appoint him as a successor. Both of these claims are blatantly baseless. Yet, even if we assume for the sake of argument that the event of Ghadīr Khumm never took place, we have enough evidence to deduce his rightful succession to the Holy Prophet. The Holy Prophet would tell Imam ʿAlī,

لا يحبك إلا مؤمن و لا يبغضك الا منافق

None but a believer will love you. None but a hypocrite will hate you.[1]

The Holy Prophet would also say,

الحق مع علي وعلي مع الحق ولن يفترقا حتى يردا علي الحوض يوم القيامة

The truth is with ʿAlī and ʿAlī is with the truth. They will not separate until they reach me at the Pond [of Paradise] on the Day of Judgement.[2]

These are just two examples of countless others. All his contemporaries seemed to agree on his great merits. The second caliph ʿUmar ibn al-Khaṭṭāb would continuously seek Imam ʿAlī's advice on issues of governance and judgement. Furthermore, Imam ʿAlī was so proficient in religious and temporal matters that ʿUmar would say, "If it were not for ʿAlī, ʿUmar would have perished!"[3] and "May God not leave me to see a problem that cannot be solved by Abū'l-Ḥasan!"[4]

The Muslims never doubted Imam ʿAlī's merits. Their issue was of a different caliber. They doubted whether authority must be vested in the most meritorious. The issue can be seen clearly in the words of ibn Abī'l-

---

[1] sl-Tirmithī, *al-Jāmiʿ al-kabīr*, 6:94.

[2] Ibn ʿAsākir, *Tārīkh dimashq*, 42:449; al-Majlisī, *Biḥār al-anwār*, 38:38.

[3] Ibn ʿAbdulbar, *al-Istīʿāb*, 1103.

[4] al-Balādhirī, *Ansāb al-ashrāf*, 2:351.

Ḥadīd, a Muʿtazilī scholar who wrote a multivolume commentary on *Nahj al-Balāghah*. He begins his book by praising God who "preferred the inferior over the superior." Many Muslims seem to believe that despite Imam ʿAlī holding the greatest merits and best qualifications, others took priority over him in the line of succession. The greater interest dictated so. From where did this priority arose? What was that greater interest? This remains a mystery.

In contemporary times, humanity's experiences have led it to a completely opposite position. The rational consensus seems to be that, when it comes to authority, we must place our trust in the hands of the most competent and qualified. That is why, for example, we place conditions on who can practice medicine and we continue to regulate the practice even after a doctor earns her license. The same is true in the civic and political sphere. Whenever a candidate gets voted into office, it is out of – or should be out of – the belief that the candidate is the most capable of serving the electorate's interest. And because the ballot box does not necessarily provide the best result and power may corrupt an individual who wields it, checks are placed on political power to ensure balance between competing authorities.

It seems that modern political philosophy has come to the conclusion that no perfectly capable and qualified individual exists to exercise this authority. Modern governments have been crafted around the idea that the governors are imperfect. During the founding of the American republic, the authors of the Federalist Papers wrote, "If angels were to govern men, neither external nor internal controls on government would be necessary."[5] Humanity has come to understand that immaculacy is the greatest qualification for authority. The only problem is that they have not yet identified the ideal fit.

These are conclusions that humanity has arrived at after centuries of experience and struggle. On the other hand, Muslim society seems stuck in the mindset of 'preferring the inferior over the superior' or turning a blind eye to the vast heritage indicating that Imam ʿAlī was indeed more qualified.

Returning to the question we asked at the outset, the answer should now be clear that naṣṣ does not limit the role of reason. The naṣṣ regarding the issue of imamate is unlike the naṣṣ surrounding the number of

[5] Madison, *the Federalist Papers*, No. 51.

bowings (*raka ʿāt*) in prayer. The latter is purely *ta ʾsisī* and *ta ʿabbudī* – it does not provide room for our intellects to attempt rationalizing why the number of *raka ʿāt* in *fajr* prayer is less than all the others. When it comes to imamate, the naṣṣ provides a clear answer to the question of successorship, but does not stop the mind from contemplating its standards and qualifications.

Four Advantages

As we have mentioned, naṣṣ carries a great deal of weight as a means of establishing truth and legitimacy. That is because the naṣṣ evidences a divine proclamation in a specific manner. Namely, naṣṣ gives us four advantages over other types of evidence.

Devotion

First, divine pronouncements are a form of legislation from a position of authority which adds a layer of moral imperatives to the subject. Whenever naṣṣ exists, it obliges us to observe its dictates out of devotion (*ta ʿabbud*) to God Almighty.

Let us consider prayer as an illustrative example. On numerous occasions, we have been commanded by God and His messenger to 'establish prayers.' The fact that God obligated us to pray and emphasized its importance can lead us to make the following conclusion: that prayer holds such great benefits that God instructed us to pray out of His limitless mercy and grace.

Now let us assume that God never commanded us to pray. Instead, he informed us of the indispensable benefits of prayer. A rational individual would not forgo his self interest if he knows that a small daily time commitment would result in such great rewards. Knowing these benefits, we would rationally take on prayer as a daily obligation.[6]

In both the example and the hypothetical, we know that prayer is an obligation that must be fulfilled. However, there is no question that in the first instance, God's explicit commands creates an added layer of moral obligation. This is because of His divine and moral authority over us, as He has blessed us and continues to bless us with His infinite graces.

---

[6] The study of *uṣūl al-fiqh* addresses a plethora of topics regarding derivation of religious rulings. Can we rationally deduce the obligatory nature of an action without explicit divine command? Can we be lenient in weighing evidence of recommended acts? When are obligatory precaution and recommended precaution to be utilized? All these topics are far too detailed to address in this short treatise.

In another example, suppose that a smoker is speaking to a doctor after his annual checkup. The doctor instructs the smoker to quit smoking, listing all the negative health effects that it causes. In fact, the doctor says, 'If you don't quit smoking, you will develop lung cancer and die in a year.' Knowing the severe harms of smoking would oblige him to quit, even though the doctor has no legal or moral authority over the patient. Now suppose that the patient's father is sitting beside him while the doctor spoke. He begins to cry and pleads with his son that he should quit smoking. The father commands his son to quit smoking at once. By knowing the consequences of his actions, his reason deduced that he must quit smoking. However, the father's command adds a layer of moral obligation over that of the rational obligation.

When the naṣṣ evidences a divine proclamation commanding humanity to act in a certain way, there is a heightened level of obligation because it comes from a position of authority. Contemplating that authority will invoke a greater sense of duty to comply with that command. To contemplate the attributes of God will strengthen that sense of duty.

هُوَ اللَّهُ الَّذِي لَا إِلَٰهَ إِلَّا هُوَ الْمَلِكُ الْقُدُّوسُ السَّلَامُ الْمُؤْمِنُ الْمُهَيْمِنُ الْعَزِيزُ الْجَبَّارُ الْمُتَكَبِّرُ ۚ سُبْحَانَ اللَّهِ عَمَّا يُشْرِكُونَ

He is God, other than whom there is no god – [He is] the Sovereign, the Holy, Peace, the Faithful, the Protector, the Mighty, the Compeller, the Proud. Glory be to God above the partners they ascribe.[7]

This is all because obedience to God – after knowing Him and His attributes – is of the highest and most basic goals of practical reason. As the believer grows in faith and understanding, its centrality in his life becomes more and more evident. The Commander of the Faithful speaks to the Almighty and says,

إلهي ما عبدتك خوفا من عقابك ولا طمعا في ثوابك، ولكن وجدتك أهلا للعبادة فعبدتك

God! I did not worship You due to fear of Your punishment nor due to a yearning for Your rewards. Rather, I found You to be worthy of worship, and so I worship You![8]

[7] The Holy Qur'an, 59:23.

[8] al-Majlisī, *Biḥār al-anwār*, 41:14.

For a true believer of this caliber, the worldly blessings guaranteed through obedience become trivial. The matters of otherworldly reward and punishment become secondary. The true driving force becomes the sense of duty and gratitude towards the most sublime and Almighty Lord.

Scope

Second, naṣṣ can provide a broader and more instructive form of evidence. For example, reason permits us to conclude with certainty that justice is good and that oppression is evil. However, we cannot say that we have comprehensively analyzed all possible reasons for justice's goodness or for oppression's evil. We can say that justice is good in itself and because it allows us to establish lasting social order. But what of the spiritual and metaphysical aspects of justice? Those are beyond reason's purview. We need naṣṣ to provide us a vision of those aspects of reality.

Thus, naṣṣ can allow us to reach conclusions that reliance on pure rational argumentation cannot. We have seen how rational analysis can lead us to the necessity of an imam and his role within a wider worldview. However, rational analysis cannot lead us to conclusions about the imams' role within an otherworldly purview. The mind cannot analytically derive the sublime positions of creational authority, religious authority, witness over the deeds of mankind, and the like. Naṣṣ can give us insight that we cannot arrive at otherwise.[9]

In addition, reason alone allows us to reach general principles, but it cannot alone dictate specifics. It tells us that justice is good, but it does not allow us to always know what justice is in every situation.

Naṣṣ in identifying the imam provides evidence of aspects and details of imamate that reason alone cannot reach, while at the same time allowing reason to reach its general and consistent conclusions about the subject.

Reach

Third, there are three types of communication that can be used to address a population.

Philosophical communication addresses theoretical reason and is essential in establishing rational frameworks. However, this type of

[9] Moreover, while reason allows us to conclude the necessity of prophets and imams, we need naṣṣ to identify who these specific individuals are.

communication is not easily understood and is often reserved for the experts in a specific field.

Practical communication is the language of practical reason and is broader and more easily understood. This is why Islamic theology uses practical as opposed to philosophical arguments. To solidify and defend people's faith, a language must be used that is better understood by the masses.

Legal communication is the broadest and can be understood by all people. It is the language of rules, of 'do' and 'do not.'

On general questions, we cannot guarantee that people will respond positively to philosophical communication. To be effective, the simplest language – legal communication – must be used. The layman will not need to expend time and effort understanding intricate philosophical questions. He will only need to take the advice of the expert.

What if we only present the reasons why a certain action should or should not be taken? It will not be enough to ensure that a society will operate in the most uniform way, as opposed to the results of legal communication. Society might also not be able to understand how to apply those instructions. Society is more likely to conform to the commands of law than the prudence of reason.

For example, contemporary societies place great restrictions on the manufacture and use of pharmaceuticals – a system formalized by law and regulation. We cannot use philosophical communication because we cannot expect all people in a society to become doctors or pharmacists, knowing every pharmaceutical compound and its effects. Neither can we regulate society simply by informing people that there are a set of drugs – like opioids – that are harmful and should not be used unless absolutely necessary. The most effective means of ensuring society's health and safety is by a system of legal regulations, where some drugs are prohibited and others are permitted.

This does not mean that philosophical and practical communication are not necessary, not useful, or not conclusive. However, philosophical and practical communication have a narrower use in effecting the actions of a population. They need detailed study and continued scrutiny, something not easily attainable to each individual in society. Societies cannot effectively regulate themselves with philosophical and practical arguments. Societies need laws.

The language of law is a shared language understood by all. Naṣṣ is divine declaration – a divine legal communication. It saves us from having to dedicate the time and energy of each one of us in order to understand the intricacies of philosophical and practical communications.

The foregoing allows us to better understand the benefits of naṣṣ in identifying the imam. Theoretical and practical reason may be able to identify the individual, but only after gaining expertise in the relevant sciences and studying the evidence in great depth. This is not possible for every single member of society to achieve. Naṣṣ gives us a shortcut, allowing us to reach the rational conclusion without dedicating so much time and effort to the endeavor. The result is certainty derived more easily, and perhaps at a level even greater, than relying on practical reason alone.

We do not mean to belittle the rationality and reasonableness of laymen. They are rational individuals utilizing their intellectual resources to reach rational conclusions. The problem is in applying rational principles to specific instances, a process that is long, arduous, and perilous. Laymen cannot demand to know the rational and prudential reasonings behind every intricate detail of religion – or any other subject for that matter. These details did not come at the stroke of a pen. They are the result of centuries of rigorous study and debate. The road is not closed to anyone. All we ask is that if someone wishes to know the details of every answers, they must dedicate their life to becoming an expert in the field.

Centrality

Fourth, divine pronouncements are of a higher order than other sources of obligation. Consider the following example. You receive a letter informing you that you are in violation of city ordinances and advising you that you may be fined if you do not take corrective action. This letter is of legal nature and you are bound to act accordingly. Is there a difference if the violation was of a provincial or state law? What about if the violation was of a federal law? What if the supreme court of the land found you to be in violation of your country's constitution? In all these examples, you are in receipt of a legal document informing you of your duty to take a certain course of action. However, the weight of that duty differs based on its origin.

The same is true with religious obligations. Though we may label a variety of actions as obligatory or forbidden, they are of different significances and levels. We regard God's admonishment to 'establish prayer' with greater weight than a jurist's verdict on whether we must recite with a low or high tone during prayer. Again, the different weight we give to each is based on its origin.

God commanded the Holy Prophet to inform the Muslims of Imam ʿAlī's appointment as successor.

يَا أَيُّهَا الرَّسُولُ بَلِّغْ مَا أُنزِلَ إِلَيْكَ مِن رَّبِّكَ ۖ وَإِن لَّمْ تَفْعَلْ فَمَا بَلَّغْتَ رِسَالَتَهُ

> *Apostle! Communicate that which has been sent down to you from your Lord, and if you do not, you will not have communicated His message.*[10]

Does this appointment hold the same weight as Imam ʿAlī's appointment of Mālik al-Ashtar as governor of Egypt? They are both commands that must be followed. Yet the former is of a higher order because of its origin. Comparing the two is like comparing a constitutional provision with a presidential proclamation – although they are both legally binding, the former is of a higher order than the latter.

To say that there is naṣṣ regarding imamate is to show the great weight and centrality of the concept to the religious framework.

If we look deeper into the naṣṣ, we find it to be clear on this issue. It is narrated that Imam al-Ṣādiq said,

لعلكم ترون أن هذا الأمر في الإمامة إلى الرجل منا يضعه حيث يشاء، والله إنه لعهد من الله نزل على رسول الله (صلى الله عليه وآله) إلى رجال مسمين رجل فرجل حتى تنتهي إلى صاحبها

> *Perhaps you believe that the matter of imamate is in the hands of each of us to place wherever he wishes? By God, it is rather a covenant from God delivered to the Messenger of God for men named one after the other until it reaches [the promised Mahdī].*[11]

There would be no issue if succession in imamate was left to the choice of the preceding imam. Just as we accept their teachings and guidance in all matters, we accept it here as well. But the imam wished to inform his followers that the issue of imamate is of such great importance that God Almighty made it a covenant upon the Holy Prophet, naming each

---

[10] The Holy Qurʾan, 5:67.

[11] al-Nuʿmānī, *al-Ghaybah*, 59.

of his successors by name. When the Holy Prophet made this covenant abundantly clear to the Muslims, God declared the religion of Islam finally complete.

الْيَوْمَ أَكْمَلْتُ لَكُمْ دِينَكُمْ وَأَتْمَمْتُ عَلَيْكُمْ نِعْمَتِي وَرَضِيتُ لَكُمُ الْإِسْلَامَ دِينًا

Today I have perfected your religion for you, and I have completed My blessing upon you, and I have approved Islam as your religion.[12]

A person who does not know and follow the imam of his time has not truly followed that religion which God perfected and approved. That is why the narrations state that ignorance of the imam is ignorance of Islam.

من مات ولم يعرف إمام زمانه مات ميتة جاهلية

Whoever passes not knowing the imam of his time has passed [as if he were still in] the Age of Ignorance.[13]

It is not just that any imam must be followed – there are specific qualities and qualifications. God declares,

إِنَّمَا وَلِيُّكُمُ اللَّهُ وَرَسُولُهُ وَالَّذِينَ آمَنُوا الَّذِينَ يُقِيمُونَ الصَّلَاةَ وَيُؤْتُونَ الزَّكَاةَ وَهُمْ رَاكِعُونَ

Your guardian is only Allah, His Apostle, and the faithful who maintain the prayer and give the zakat while bowing down.[14]

This all indicates the central and incontrovertible standing of imamate. The Holy Qurʾan is rich with verses speaking of the issue, both patently and latently. The noble traditions are no less familiar with the issue. Our continued emphasis on the existence of naṣṣ in regards to imamate is not just to say that the evidence exists, but to highlight its importance and centrality.

Reassessing the Alternatives to Naṣṣ

To fully understand the meaning of having naṣṣ in support of an imam, we must first recognize that there are two dimensions from which we can understand the naṣṣ's purpose.

---

[12] The Holy Qurʾan, 5:3.

[13] al-Majlisī, *Biḥār al-anwār*, 32:321. This narration is present, albeit with slightly different wording, in the major Sunni books of tradition. See, for example: al-Naysābūrī, *Ṣaḥīḥ Muslim*, 898; ibn Ḥanbal, *Musnad Aḥmad*, 28:88.

[14] The Holy Qurʾan, 5:55.

First, the naṣṣ comes as a means of establishing legitimacy. The fact that a divine declaration exists appointing an individual as successor to a prophet gives that individual direct legitimacy. In fact, if we look at the *nuṣūṣ* in question, we find that they are explicit in stating that the appointment of a successor is an issue of divine choice and will. It was not delegated to the Holy Prophet to choose his successor,[15] let alone to the ummah to choose its leader. Once a divine pronouncement is made on any issue, the role of the Muslims is simply to follow. When God appointed the Holy Prophet's successor and commanded His prophet to announce it to the Muslims, it was not up to them to choose a different leader. Their duty was to follow that command and allow the appointed successor to take his rightful place in leading the Muslim ummah – not just politically, but in all other facets of their life.

Second, naṣṣ serves a revelatory and demonstrative purpose. It points out to the Muslims the individuals amongst them who were able to mold their character and their spirits to be able to accept God's most cherished gifts. Naṣṣ reveals the merits and character of the imam, showcasing his unique status and his possession of that particular knowledge that qualifies him to hold the most supreme positions.

As we have mentioned before, even if we assume for the sake of argument that no evidence of a divine appointment exists, we may still be able to use reason to draw the outlines of imamate. However, we cannot fill in every detail with reason alone. Reason must rely on the proper evidence to identify the individual who possesses the qualities of particular knowledge, immaculacy, creational authority, and *al-hidāyah al-iyṣāliyyah*. Such qualities cannot normally be reached by our normal senses and faculties. To identify these divinely endowed supernatural traits, we must rely on naṣṣ to aid our reason.

The result is that naṣṣ does not inhibit or limit human reason. However, reason is only useful as a 'Plan B' – the assumed scenario where naṣṣ does not exist or is rejected. Even then, reason does not provide the same advantages that naṣṣ does.

Reason can conclude that temporal imamate is best suited for an immaculate, or that the imam is the most knowledgeable. However, reason

---

[15] Even if it were delegated to the Holy Prophet, he is immaculate and makes the choice that God would want.

cannot identify divinely appointed imamate – naṣṣ is the only true indication of that.

But whether we rely on naṣṣ or reason only, the supposed alternatives to naṣṣ remain untenable. The assumption of the absence of naṣṣ would not mean that legitimacy can be seized by or granted to anyone, regardless of qualifications. It would not mean that we must submit to a fiat, accepting the dictates of history without question.

Reason alone can identify the outlines of imamate. It can conclude that God Almighty, in His justice and grace, would not leave us without an imam. It can even identify the imam by relying on the proper evidence, such as the traditions dictating the merits of Imam ʿAlī.

The assumed absence of naṣṣ does not justify a fiat approach to imamate. Reason continues to dictate the proper qualifications of a leader. Even in the absence of that, we can look at *sīrat al-ʿuqalāʾ* (the "custom of the reasonable") to identify the rational course. Absent that, we can take rational precautions and choose the most meritorious to lead the ummah.

Never would reason lead to arbitrary selection, fiat theories of legitimacy, or elections with indifference to candidate's traits and qualifications.

This line of thinking is also supported by naṣṣ. As one tradition of the Holy Prophet states,

من استعمل غلاما في عصابة فيها من هو أرضى لله منه فقد خان الله

> *Whoever appoints a leader to a group knowing that there is someone amongst them who would be more pleasing to God than him, he has surely betrayed God.*[16]

ʿAllāmah al-Majlisī categorizes this tradition within the chapter specified for 'the necessity of existence of naṣṣ.' Why? What does this tradition have to do with divine appointment of a leader through naṣṣ?

This tradition is loaded with connotations in regard to leadership, appointment, and naṣṣ. The tradition states that the individual who is most pleasing to God, the one who is able to lead righteously and implement justice, should be allowed to assume the position of leadership. When we look to the imams from the Holy Household, we find that they hold the greatest qualities and qualifications. They are surely the most

[16] al-Majlisī, *Biḥār al-anwār*, 23:75.

pleasing to God. Their knowledge and qualifications don't stop at the spiritual but encompass all other aspects of life. Why would we choose anyone else?

This tradition is explicit in stating that 'preferring the inferior over the superior' is as much a betrayal to God as it is a betrayal to human reason.

Naṣṣ and Spirit

The foregoing discussion has centered on naṣṣ and reason, and the uses and advantages of naṣṣ over reason.

When reading the *nuṣūṣ* in this regard, we find that they help in setting a foundation for the rational approach to imamate. They also set the foundation for a spiritual approach to imamate. It is a concept that can be savored by anyone with a sound heart and spirit.

Jābir ibn ʿAbdullāh al-Anṣārī narrates the following event from the mosque of the Holy Prophet. He says that a delegation from Yemen came to visit the Messenger of God. When they entered, he began to praise them saying,

> قوم رقيقة قلوبهم راسخ إيمانهم، منهم المنصور يخرج في سبعين ألفا ينصر خلفي وخلف وصيي
>
> *These are a people of soft hearts and deep-rooted faith. From them is al-manṣūr [the divinely-supported] who will set out with seventy thousand to support my successor and the successor of my viceroy...*

They rejoiced when they heard this praise, but were left wondering who the Holy Prophet's viceroy was. When they asked, the Holy Prophet responded,

> هو الذي أمركم الله بالاعتصام به فقال عز وجل ﴿واعتصموا بحبل الله جميعا ولا تفرقوا﴾
>
> *He is the one who God commanded you to hold fast to when He said, 'Hold fast, all together, to Allah's rope, and do not be divided.'* [17]

They asked the Holy Prophet about this rope, to which he replied,

> هو قول الله ﴿إلا بحبل من الله وحبل من الناس﴾، فالحبل من الله كتابه، والحبل من الناس وصيي

[17] The Holy Qurʾan, 3:103.

It is in the words of God, 'except for a rope from God and a rope from the people.' [18] *The rope from God is His book, and the rope from the people is my viceroy.*

They continued to ask and the Holy Prophet continued to recite verses of the Holy Qur'an pertaining to his viceroy. Finally, the delegation pleaded, "Messenger of God! By Him who sent you with truth as a prophet, show him to us. Surely, we are longing to see him." The Holy Prophet replied,

هو الذي جعله الله آية المتوسمين، فإن نظرتم إليه نظر من كان له قلب أو ألقى السمع وهو شهيد عرفتم أنه وصيي كما عرفتم إني نبيكم، فتخللوا الصفوف وتصفحوا الوجوه فمن أهوت إليه قلوبكم فإنه هو، إن الله عز وجل يقول في كتابه ﴿فاجعل أفئدة من الناس تهوي إليهم﴾

He is the one who God made as a sign to the perceptive. If you were to look upon him with the insight of those with heart or who give ear with full attention, you will know him to be my viceroy as you know me to be your prophet. Go through the lines and look upon these faces. Whomever you find your hearts to be fond of, he is surely him. God Almighty says in His book, 'So make the hearts of a part of the people fond of them.' [19]

The leaders of the delegation stood up and began to walk through the lines of Muslims at the mosque. After a moment, they took the hands of a man and proclaimed, "Messenger of God! We find our hearts to be fond of this man!" The Holy Prophet responded,

أنتم نخبة الله حين عرفتم وصي رسول الله قبل أن تعرفوه، فبم عرفتم أنه هو؟

You are the select servants of God, having known the viceroy of the Messenger of God before you were introduced to him. How did you know that it was him?

They wept and said,

We looked at these people, but our hearts were not yearning towards of any of them. Yet when we saw him, our hearts raced, our spirits calmed, our stomachs turned, our eyes teared, and our chests cooled. It was as if he was our father and we were his sons!

The Holy Prophet joyfully gave them glad tidings,

---

[18] The Holy Qur'an, 3:112.

[19] The Holy Qur'an, 14:37.

وما يعلم تأويله إلا الله والراسخون في العلم، أنتم منه بالمنزلة التي سبقت لكم بها الحسنى وأنتم عن النار مبعدون

Surely, no one knows its interpretation except Allah and those firmly grounded in knowledge! In relation to them, you are in the station - because of which - for you there has gone beforehand [the promise of] the best reward from Us and you shall be kept away from the Hellfire.[20]

As we have mentioned, the naṣṣ acts to reveal and demonstrate an existing reality. The delegation from Yemen did not need naṣṣ in order to find the imam. Instead, they relied on his divinely endowed charisma which drew their hearts and spirits to him. His *hidāyah iyṣāliyyah* worked to deliver guidance to them, as their hearts and spirits were receptive to it. Naṣṣ about imamate reveals a truth sought by the human heart, mind, and soul.

Of course, this type of spiritual evidence is not available to all. In fact, it can be deeply flawed and may create much misguidance if it is not exercised within its proper limits and safeguards. The only reason we know that the Yemeni delegation were able to accurately identify the imam is because the Holy Prophet was there to guide and oversee the process. Moreover, the spiritual evidence that they felt could not be transferred or demonstrated to anyone else. It remains evidence for them and not for others.

The Yemeni delegation was able to make an accurate choice through spiritual evidence. How do we know that such evidence is not fabricated or imagined? Such evidence is not measurable or verifiable in any ordinary way. No ordinary human being can probe the hearts and spirits of others. As with any type of evidence, there needs to be a rigorous methodology that allows us to evaluate potential spiritual evidence that we may feel in our hearts and spirits. Additionally, such spiritual evidence cannot be generalized as legitimate proof for anyone other than those who possessed it in their hearts.

The Yemeni delegation had the blessing of having the Holy Prophet attest to the truth of their spiritual evidence. The presence and words of the Holy Prophet provided them with naṣṣ in support of their spiritually guided choice. This gave generalizable validity to their spiritual

[20] al-Nuʿmānī, *al-Ghaybah*, 46.

evidence – the proof for us is not what they felt in their spirits, but the naṣṣ of the Holy Prophet.

Thus, although we may be able to use reason, spiritual evidence, or other means to identify the imam, these tools are not the proper tools for the general masses. Naṣṣ is the best form of evidence in proving divine dictates to a broader population.

All this is to say that our attachment to naṣṣ is not because it is the only epistemological tool at our disposal. It is rooted in our belief that appointment of a successor is a matter of divine will. Divine will may be evidenced by miracles, reason, spiritual evidence, or naṣṣ. That is because naṣṣ in regard to imamate was not completely devotional (*taʿabbudī*). It provided context and space for us to utilize our hearts and minds to reach the same conclusion. However, naṣṣ remains the superior method of evidence due to the multiple dimensions and advantages that it provides.

Summarising Naṣṣ

In this and the previous chapter, we have discussed some of the theoretical and practical implications of the Shia approach to naṣṣ.

In short, naṣṣ has multiple meanings, and it is a necessity in more than one of its meanings. Naṣṣ is a necessity as divine pronouncement and as evidence thereof. Naṣṣ also provides the framework, context, and space for us to utilize our hearts and minds and reach the proper conclusion. Yet it is a more useful and proper form of evidence than the rational and spiritual.

The countless prophetic traditions about Imam ʿAlī also provide us with an understanding of his specific traits and characteristics, allowing us to draw a more detailed picture about the qualifications and position of imamate.

The Shia school of thought sifted through all the evidence – naṣṣ, reason, practical principles (*al-uṣūl al-ʿamaliyyah*),[21] and spiritual evidence. They all resulted in the same conclusion about imamate and the imam. They also excluded the following alternatives: (a) the primacy of popular opinion, regardless of the individual's qualifications or their faithful

---

[21] *al-uṣūl al-ʿamaliyyah* is a major focus of the study of *uṣūl al-fiqh*. It addresses the practical principles applied when the religious evidence is absent or inconclusive. For example, see: al-Muẓaffar, *Uṣūl al-fiqh*, volume 4.

execution of duty; and (b) the philosophies that saw legitimacy starting at the time that the individual fills the role of caliph.

The Shia emphasis on naṣṣ was also an emphasis on divine commands and teachings, ensuring that the imam is the most knowledgeable of and compliant with the divine will.

OUR RESPONSIBILITY

We have been speaking thus far of what the concept of imamate means to the followers of the Holy Household. We have analyzed the issue at length, looking at the Holy Qur'an and noble traditions to glean a clearer understanding of that concept's role in our faith. Now, we must turn to ourselves and ask the following question: what is our role and responsibility towards this concept and those who embodied it?

Imamate and Tawḥīd

When we read the Holy Qur'an and the noble tradition, we find great emphasis on the connection between imamate and *tawḥīd* – the monotheistic belief in God and His attributes. So much so that any error in an individual's belief in and duty towards imamate is described as an error in the belief and practice of tawḥīd. Our responsibility towards imamate and tawḥīd are not like our obligation of prayer and fasting. Prayer and fasting are two independent obligations. An individual's error in or neglect of prayer does not invalidate his fast, and vice versa. When we look at the noble traditions describing imamate and tawḥīd, we find them to be significantly interdependent. There are many points that we can highlight regarding this perspective. For the sake of brevity, we will suffice ourselves with this non-exhaustive list of seven points.

First, the belief of tawḥīd is identified and affirmed through the imam. The imam teaches us what tawḥīd means in its most accessible forms. That is why the imams emphasized that it was through their grandfather the Holy Prophet and through them that God was known and worshiped. Imam al-Bāqir said,

> بنا عبد الله، وبنا عرف الله، وبنا وحد الله تبارك وتعالى، ومحمد حجاب الله تبارك وتعالى
>
> *Through us, God was worshiped. Through us, God was known. Through us, God Almighty was known to be One. Muḥammad is the veil of God Almighty.*[1]

By "the veil of God," Imam al-Bāqir means that the Holy Prophet is the intermediary through which God sends us His blessings and mercy. It is through the message delivered by the Holy Prophet and the guidance provided by his family that God continues to be worshipped on this Earth. However, this Holy Family shouldered this burden and faced great tribulations because of it. As Imam al-Ṣādiq said,

> بلية الناس عظيمة إن دعوناهم لم يجيبونا ، وإن تركناهم لم يهتدوا بغيرنا
>
> *The test of the people [and how we are to deal with them] is formidable; if we call them, they do not answer, and if we leave them, they will not be guided by any other than us!* [2]

From this Holy Household, divine knowledge and immaculate character emanated to the rest of the world. As we read in a noble tradition that we have cited above,

> ليس عند أحد من الناس حق ولا صواب ولا أحد من الناس يقضي بقضاء حق إلا ما خرج منا أهل البيت
>
> *No individual possesses any truth or correct [understanding], nor is there any individual that administers a just judgement, except what comes from us Ahl al-Bayt.*[3]

Second, the imams show us what the deepest and most sincere form of tawḥīd looks like. You find most of the schools of Islamic mysticism claim to hold Imam ʿAlī as its leader – though many of them have diverted from his path. Imam ʿAlī's life and teachings hold some of the most vivid examples of devotion and servility to the Almighty.

Third, belief in imamate and devotion to the imams represent true sincerity in tawḥīd. The following narrations illustrate the point. The Holy Prophet said,

---

[1] al-Kulaynī, *al-Kāfī*, 1:145.

[2] al-Majlisī, *Biḥār al-anwār*, 23:99.

[3] al-Kulaynī, *al-Kāfī*, 1:399.

إن لا إله إلا الله كلمة عظيمة كريمة على الله عز وجل، من قالها مخلصا استوجب الجنة

> *'There is no god but God' is a great and honorable word in the view of God Almighty. Paradise becomes due to whoever says it sincerely.*[4]

An Arab nomad once asked the Holy Prophet about the price of eternal life in Paradise. The Holy Prophet said,

لا إله إلا الله، يقولها العبد مخلصا بها

> *'There is no god but God,' said sincerely by a servant.*

The nomad asked, "And how is it said sincerely?" The Holy Prophet responded,

العمل بما بعثت به في حقه وحب أهل بيتي

> *To implement the message with which I have been sent in respect to Him, as well as love towards my household.*

The first portion is obvious. The best translation of an individual's sincerity in implementing the message of tawḥīd is following the Messenger's teachings. A deficiency on that part could be a result of the individual's insincerity. Still, the nomad was surprised by the second part. He asked, "And is love towards your household part of its due right?" The Holy Prophet answered,

إن حبهم لأعظم حقها

> *Surely, their love is the greatest of its due right!*[5]

Imam al-Riḍā was asked a similar question to which he responded,

طاعة الله ورسوله وولاية أهل بيته

> *Obedience to God and His messenger, and devotion to his household.*[6]

Notice that the imam did not say that sincerity in tawḥīd was simply obedience to the Holy Household. Instead, *tawallī* to them is the key. We will address the concept of tawallī in more detail in the next chapter.

Fourth, deeper awareness of the Imam is a way to deeper awareness of God's attributes. The more we know the Imam, the more we know God's

---

[4] al-Ṣadūq, *al-Tawḥīd*, 23.

[5] al-Majlisī, *Biḥār al-anwār*, 27:136.

[6] Ibid.

attributes and grace. This knowledge of God is the first matter that God commanded His creation to observe. Imam al-Riḍā said,

إن أول ما افترض الله على عباده وأوجب على خلقه معرفة الوحدانية قال الله تبارك وتعالى: ﴿وما قدروا الله حق قدره﴾. يقول: ما عرفوا الله حق معرفته

The first matter that God obliged His servants with and compelled His creations towards, is to know His Oneness. God Almighty says, 'They did not regard God with the regard due to Him.' Meaning that they did not know God with the knowledge that is due to Him.[7]

If we connect this narration to the ones we have read above, we can conclude that through imamate we come closer to sincerely recognizing and being aware of God's Oneness. This is because to know them is to know the greatness of God's blessings and grace. As the Commander of the Faithful used to say,

ما لله عز وجل آية هي أكبر مني

There is no sign of God greater than me.[8]

All this allows us to understand the following narration. Imam al-Ḥusayn was asked, "What is it to know God?" He replied,

معرفة أهل كل زمان إمامهم الذي يجب عليهم طاعته

It is for the people of each era to know their imam whom they are obliged to obey.[9]

Al-Shaykh al-Ṣadūq comments on this narration and states,

By this, he means that the people of each era should know that God will not leave them at any time without an immaculate imam. Whoever worships a lord who does not establish for them this proof has worshipped something other than God Almighty.[10]

The reader should note the distinction between this point and the first. We spoke above about their role in identifying what tawḥīd is to the masses. Here, we come to a deeper understanding – a much higher and sublime connection between imamate and tawḥīd. These noble traditions clarify that to be deeply aware of the imam is to be deeply aware

---

7 al-Majlisī, *Biḥār al-anwār*, 3:13.

8 al-Kulaynī, *al-Kāfī*, 1:207.

9 al-Majlisī, *Biḥār al-anwār*, 23:83.

10 Ibid.

of God – to know the imam is to know God. Our knowledge of the two is so interconnected that we cannot claim to know one without knowing the other.

Fifth, imamate represents the safeguard which ensures the preservation of tawḥīd. Our beliefs and good deeds are not singular actions that are done and earned, but they must be maintained and safeguarded until the Day of Judgement. God says in His holy book,

مَن جَاءَ بِالْحَسَنَةِ فَلَهُ خَيْرٌ مِّنْهَا وَهُم مِّن فَزَعٍ يَوْمَئِذٍ آمِنُونَ

> *Whoever brings virtue shall receive [a reward] better than it; and on that day they will be secure from terror.*[11]

It is not enough to act virtuously. Rather, that virtue must be maintained until it can be brought forth on that day. We must ensure that our hearts become an 'eternal abode' of faith and virtue, and not just a 'temporary lodging' of those characteristics.[12] We can find many examples in history of individuals that were held in the highest esteem due to their faith, but who then deviated to become of the most wretched out of pride, greed, and envy. Even some close companions of the Holy Prophet and the Immaculate Imams fell into that trap. The most vivid example of that is Satan himself who, as we are told by narrations, was one of the most devout worshippers. According to Imam ʿAlī,

فَاعْتَبِرُوا بِمَا كَانَ مِنْ فِعْلِ اللهِ بِإِبْلِيسَ، إِذْ أَحْبَطَ عَمَلَهُ الطَّوِيلَ، وَجَهْدَهُ الْجَهِيدَ، وَكَانَ قَدْ عَبَدَ اللهَ سِتَّةَ آلاَفِ سَنَة، لاَ يُدْرَى أَمِنْ سِنِي الدُّنْيَا أَمْ مِنْ سِنِي الأخِرَةِ، عَنْ كِبْرِ سَاعَة وَاحِدَة

> *You should take a lesson from what God did with Satan. He nullified his great acts and extensive efforts, although Satan had worshipped God for six thousand years – whether by the reckoning of this world or of the next world is not known – all on account of the vanity of one moment.*[13]

We must ensure that our base tendencies and regressive desires do not destroy the faith and virtue that we strive so hard to achieve and maintain.

---

[11] The Holy Qur'an, 27:89.

[12] See: The Holy Qur'an, 6:98. For more on the exegesis of this verse and its implications, see: al-Ṭabāṭabā'ī, *al-Mīzān*.

[13] al-Raḍī, *Nahj al-balāghah*, Sermon 192.

Of course, we must also realize the importance of our faith and the role that it plays in our salvation. Imam al-Ṣādiq had the following conversation with Abān ibn Taghlib, a close companion. The imam said,

إذا كان يوم القيامة نادى مناد: من شهد أن لا إله إلا الله فليدخل الجنة

On the Day of Resurrection a caller will call, 'Whosoever had witnessed that there is no god but God, let them enter Paradise!'

Abān was shocked. He asked, "Then why do people dispute [the issues of faith] if it were that whosoever had witnessed that there is no god but God enters Paradise?" Imam al-Ṣādiq said,

إنه إذا كان يوم القيامة نسوها

On the Day of Resurrection, they shall forget it.[14]

In another instance, Imam al-Ṣādiq instructed Abān to narrate this tradition to the people of Kufa.

يا أبان إذا قدمت الكوفة فارو هذا الحديث: من شهد أن لا إله إلا الله مخلصا وجبت له الجنة.

Abān! When you reach Kufa, narrate this tradition: whosoever witnesses that there is no god but God with sincerity, Paradise has become his due.

Abān, who was a scholar and a notable individual in Kufa, would be visited by people of all shades and colors. He thought that if he were to narrate this tradition, it might give them a false sense of security and lead them to neglect their other obligations. He asked the imam, "I am visited by all types of people. Should I relate this tradition to them?" The imam replied,

نعم يا أبان إنه إذا كان يوم القيامة وجمع الله الأولين والآخرين فيسلب منهم لا إله إلا الله إلا من كان على هذا الامر

Yes, Abān! On the Day of Resurrection when God gathers the former and latter generation, the word of 'there is no god but God' will be stripped of all but those who are on this matter [of imamate].[15]

---

[14] al-Majlisī, *Biḥār al-anwār*, 3:12.

[15] Ibid.

Our belief in imamate and devotion to the imams is our safeguard on the Day of Judgement. It ensures that our belief in tawḥīd remains truthful until the day it allows us to enter Paradise.

Sixth, belief in imamate and tawḥīd are both part of humanity's innate nature, or *fiṭrah*. God Almighty says,

فَأَقِمْ وَجْهَكَ لِلدِّينِ حَنِيفًا فِطْرَتَ اللَّهِ الَّتِي فَطَرَ النَّاسَ عَلَيْهَا

> *So set your heart as a person of pure faith on this religion, the original nature endowed by Allah according to which He originated humanity.*[16]

In explaining this verse, Imam al-Riḍā said,

هو لا إله إلا الله ، محمد رسول الله علي أمير المؤمنين، إلى ههنا التوحيد

> *It is [the testament of] there is no god but God, Muḥammad is the messenger of God, and ʿAlī is the Commander of the Faithful. All of this is tawḥīd.*[17]

From this we understand that a rejection of imamate is a rejection of a dimension of tawḥīd and a dimension of humanity's innate nature.

Seventh, belief in imamate is an example of what our scholars call 'practical tawḥīd.' Theoretical tawḥīd – knowledge of and belief in God and His attributes – is the foundation of our faith and practice. However, we must put that theoretical understanding into practice in order to realize true faith in tawḥīd. Believing in tawḥīd must translate into action, the simplest statement of which is obedience to the commands of God. Thus, disobedience is a fault in practical tawḥīd. That is why Imam al-Ṣādiq said,

لا يزني الزاني وهو مؤمن، ولا يسرق السارق وهو مؤمن، وإنما أعني ما دام على بطنها، فإذا توضأ وتاب كان في حال غير ذلك

> *A fornicator does not fornicate while he is a believer. A thief does not steal while he is a believer. Surely, I mean that it is so while he is in the act. If he performs wuḍūʾ and repents, then he is in a different state.*[18]

An individual's disobedience of God's commands, with knowledge of who he is disobeying, is a form of practical disbelief. In order for our

---

[16] The Holy Qurʾan, 30:30.

[17] al-Majlisī, *Biḥār al-anwār*, 3:277.

[18] Ibid, 66:179.

belief in God to be real and practical, we must abide by His judgement and command. He says,

يَا أَيُّهَا الَّذِينَ آمَنُوا أَطِيعُوا اللَّهَ وَأَطِيعُوا الرَّسُولَ وَأُولِي الْأَمْرِ مِنكُمْ

O You who have faith! Obey Allah and obey the Apostle and those vested with authority among you.[19]

If nothing else, obedience to the imams is a form of practical tawḥīd because of God's command that we should follow and obey them. Of course, we first need to know who these individuals are before we can properly obey them.

From the entirety of the previous discussion, we can begin to understand the meaning of the narrations that liken those who do not follow a divinely appointed imam to those who lived in the Age of Ignorance before Islam. Imam al-Bāqir said,

من أصبح من هذه الأمة لا إمام له من الله عز وجل ظاهرا عادلا أصبح ضالا تائها

Whoever of this ummah comes to be without an evident and just imam from God Almighty, he comes to be lost and astray.[20]

These types of traditions showcase the significance of having an imam and role model who is appointed by God to guide towards the straight path.

The followers of the Holy Household suffered greatly to remain holding steadfast to their faith and their imams. They endured harassment, oppression, loss of livelihood, and all other types of persecution in order to hold on to this great heritage. We must be cognizant of the value of this legacy and hold on to it with the zeal that it deserves.

The Misconception of Impracticality

We hear at times, especially from educated friends and acquaintances, an interesting proposition about how scholars and experts in religious sciences should focus their studies. The suggestions categorize theological discussions into practical and theoretical theology. Practical theology deals with theological and religious issues with a direct and felt impact on the individual lives of the believers. This could include issues pertaining to religious unity and coexistence, or issues directly related to the family and moral decision making. Theoretical theology, on the

---

[19] The Holy Qur'an, 4:59.

[20] al-Kulaynī, *al-Kāfī*, 1:375.

other hand, handles issues of a purely conceptual and impractical nature. The focus of religious leaders should be on practical theology and not on theoretical theology.

The proponents of this opinion give numerous examples of this distinction. When it comes to the issue of imamate, they say that we should not be placing a great emphasis on the discussion of Imam ʿAlī's eminence and merit over all prophets save our Holy Prophet Muḥammad. They say that this discussion invites a great deal of hostility between us and the general Muslim public who do not ascribe to this opinion. They say that this issue causes hostility with followers of other religions – why should we claim that our imams are better than their prophets? They ask, 'What good will this discussion bring? Will you not follow Imam ʿAlī if he was not superior to Jesus, Moses, and Abraham? And if he were superior to them, will that give you any practical advantage in faith?'

There is a similar misconception which perceives theological issues as 'historical' and 'contemporary.' The claim is that many of our theological discussions – such as Imam ʿAlī's merit over all other companions – are historical in nature and do not provide us with practical benefits in our contemporary lives.

These are some examples of this misconceived proposition. The same logic is applied to theological issues beyond imamate and concerning the topics of God's attributes, prophethood, and Judgement Day. Within the topic of imamate, many similar questions are asked regarding discussions of the imams' merits and attributes. At the core, this proposition would have us focus on discussions of 'contemporary practicality,' like Muslim unity, instead of focusing on issues of mere 'historical and theoretical' importance.

We will provide two answers to this misconception, mainly to highlight the practical significance of these discussions.

First, this proposition would deprive Shiʿi Islam of its essence. It would limit our conception of imamate to a role of social and political leadership after the passing of the Holy Prophet. In effect, this would minimize our understanding of imamate to become the same as all other Muslim confessions. We will thus fall to all the inconsistencies and contradictions faced by them. We would not be able to sufficiently answer their questions about our faith. This is due to the fact that this proposition would strip away our belief in our imams' connection to the divine.

In addition, such an understanding would strip the heritage of the imams of its most important qualities. Throughout history, the followers of the Holy Household endured oppression and persecution for the sake of their dearly held belief in the imams. If we had capitulated to the popular conceptions of religious and political leadership as enforced by the ruling power, we would have saved ourselves a great deal of trouble. Yet our devotion to them meant that we would sacrifice anything to allow their teachings and legacy to live on.

That was not because the imams were merely above-average individuals. Our devotion to Imam al-Sajjād is not merely because his prayers and supplications were extraordinary. Our love for Imam al-Ḥusayn is not because he was exceptionally brave. Our dedication to Imam al-Ṣādiq is not because he knew a little more than everyone else.

Our devotion to the imams is due to their divine connection and pure souls. That is the aspect of our faith that we endured so much to preserve. Their divine connection and pure souls are the reason that their followers entrust their lives, souls, and families to them. If we are to strip our faith of that belief, we would lose an integral part of our faith.

Second, this proposition ignores the integral nature of faith generally and of these topics specifically. Religious heritage focuses on faith as the centerpiece of the religious framework. Everything else that religion came to address and regulate is secondary to faith. Knowledge, ethics, good deeds, business practices, and civilizational progress are all important but must be complementary to faith. God Almighty says in the Holy Qurʾan,

إِلَيْهِ يَصْعَدُ الْكَلِمُ الطَّيِّبُ وَالْعَمَلُ الصَّالِحُ يَرْفَعُهُ

To Him ascends the good word, and righteous conduct elevates it.[21]

The noble traditions explain that the 'good word' is faith in tawḥīd – faith in God Almighty and His divine attributes.

What is faith? Faith is defined by the Oxford English Dictionary as "complete trust or confidence in someone or something." Our scholars define it as a 'tying of the heart' on a certain matter. To have faith is higher than knowledge; a person may know something but not regard it with absolute trust in his heart. It is not only an acknowledgement in the mind,

---

[21] The Holy Qurʾan, 35:10.

but an admission through words and action. The highest levels of faith result in a complete dissolution of the self in that sincerely held belief. It is a denial of the self and its desires. It is the wellspring of all admirable characteristics.

Most importantly, faith is an integral part of the self, indistinguishable and indivisible from it. Whereas you may be able to distinguish between an individual and his actions, you cannot make that same distinction between him and his faith. Anything that is held so tightly within the individual's heart cannot be distinguished from it. It becomes an integral and defining aspect of the person's heart.

Thus, our wager as people of faith is on molding this abode of faith, this self of ours, to take us closer to God Almighty. All other topics addressed by religion – knowledge, good works, moral conduct, wealth, etc. – are for the sake of molding and purifying the self. As Imam ʿAlī wrote to his governor in Basra, after admonishing him against taking comfort in the luxuries of this world,

إِنَّمَا هِيَ نَفْسِي أَرُوضُهَا بِالتَّقْوَى

Rather, it is my self which I train through piety.[22]

Our goal and mission in this world is to train in order to transform ourselves into what allows us to ascend to the presence closest to our Lord.

This is not to say that knowledge, morality, and good works are insignificant. To the contrary, they play an immense role in this journey. However, the central and most significant attribute in all of this is faith. All the attributes that orbit around faith must always support and complement it. If they do not, faith will be undermined and will not be able to mold the spirit as it should. At the same time, if an individual holds true faith in his heart, that faith will flow through his words and actions. His conduct will be – as faith dictates – of the most sublime moral quality.

There must always be congruity between faith and action. If an individual's actions are not congruous to his faith, he has unwittingly fallen into a form of disbelief.

Having understood all this, we can see how erroneous it is to attempt to categorize issues of faith as 'practical' and 'theoretical.' Every matter of faith has its imprint, taking its place as part of the believer's most integral qualities and translating into his actions. It is senseless to say that

[22] al-Raḍī, *Nahj al-balāghah*, Letter 45.

such and such belief is impractical. Instead, the most that can be said about it is that it would translate into one form of action or another.

One must also keep in mind that our core belief system does not consist of stand-alone statements and assertions. Rather, it is a holistic model where all distinct beliefs are in fact greatly intertwined. Take, for example, the concepts of tawḥīd and imamate. The Holy Qur᾽an and noble traditions are emphatic in highlighting the connection between the two concepts. The same is true in all other major statements of our faith.

Our belief in imamate is not a mere impractical or historical issue. It is a central and formative aspect of our faith and school of thought. Without it, Shia Islam would not be Shia Islam. The same is true for other Muslim factions; their respective positions toward imamate are integral and formative to their schools of thought.

When we address these topics, it is not for intellectual sport or entertainment. We address them because we seek to understand a metaphysical aspect of our world that has a direct impact on our contemporary lives and our future, in this world and the hereafter. We seek to elucidate a part of our faith in order to strengthen it and allow it to play a greater role in our lives.

The same misconception is easier to address when it is aimed at another aspect of our faith. Take the proposition that our faith in some of God's attributes is a cause of disunity amongst humanity and an issue which cannot be empirically verified and is therefore impractical. What would happen if we limit our relationship with God to what is 'practical'? What if we say that we will consider Him as our creator and nothing further? Is this not clearly an absurd attempt to limit our faith?

The topics of immaculacy, knowledge, and creational authority, to name a few, are all important in our attempt to understand imamate and the imam. They are integral to our faith in this concept and the people who embody it. If we push aside these issues and label them as insignificant and impractical, the strength and depth of our faith would be adversely affected.

Moreover, it should be clear that the more we know about a certain topic, the higher the quality of our faith in it can become. It is one thing to believe in God out of emulation or social upbringing. It is another to believe in Him out of conviction reached through rational proofs. It is yet another when Imam ʿAlī described his faith and said,

ويلك ما كنت أعبد ربا لم أره [...] لا تدركه العيون في مشاهدة الابصار ولكن رأته القلوب بحقائق الايمان

Woe to you! Certainly, I would not worship a Lord which I have not seen! [...] He was never witnessed with the vision of the eyes, but He was seen by the hearts through the truths of faith! [23]

At the same time, we can see how different approaches to the metaphysical aspects of the Holy Prophet's character created distinctions between different schools of thought. Some schools limited their conception of his immaculacy only to his delivery of the message of Islam. The school of the Holy Household teaches that all periods and all aspects of his life have a role to play in the delivery of the message, and so his immaculacy is comprehensive.[24] These two understandings led to two distinct forms of faith in and devotion to the Holy Prophet. The attempt to paint these discussions as 'impractical' is quite practically flawed.

When an individual seeks to affirm and profess his faith, he must have a true and accurate understanding of it. If his understanding is flawed in some way, so is his faith. When we believe in the existence of a perfectly wise God, our belief is clearly different from those who believe in an arbitrary or vindictive god.

In the end, we seek to align our faith to reality and truth. If there is a mistake or omission in that, our faith will be in something other than reality – something that is false. This is the simplest statement of our answer to this misconception.

The most disheartening thing about this proposition is that it does not look at the arguments and debate the evidence. If that were the case, we would present our evidence wholeheartedly. However, the proponents of this proposition would have us cease all discussions and stop our minds from venturing into these topics. They would have us cease our intellectual and spiritual growth for the sake of their misconceived notion of 'practicality.'

Before moving on to our next topic, let us take the opportunity to ask, 'What are the roots of such a misconception?' There are numerous possibilities for the cause of such misconceptions.

---

[23] al-Kulaynī, *al-Kāfī*, 1:98.

For one, it could be the result of an understanding of religion as a purely human construct. Though few believers would profess such a worldview, the influence of such thought is evident in their words.

It could be the result of a materialistic outlook on religion. Wittingly or not, many people attempt to limit the role of the otherworldly and supernatural in their worldview.

It could be out of the misapprehension that religion imposes restrictions on the human intellect. Another possible cause is the false impression that human development accelerates once religion is removed from the picture. Such theories selectively cite history to create a skewed image of religion.

We addressed such misconceptions in a previous chapter. Let us ponder over how general critiques of religion which very few believers would ascribe to can be the origin and source of widely held misconceptions about the particulars of faith. We should ponder as such in order to make sure that we do not unintentionally accept those same assumptions which we consciously reject.

TAWALLĪ AND TABARRĪ

From the preceding discussion, we can see that acceptance of and belief in imamate necessitates a set of practical outcomes and responsibilities. As we have discussed, faith is the central piece of the religious worldview from which actions and conduct flow. At the same time, an individual's actions reaffirm and strengthen the faith that is held dearly in the heart. The set of actions that are dictated by this relationship can be described as the duties that a follower must live up to, and rights that are due to the imam.

TAWALLĪ

We often summarize this practical responsibility as tawallī, or devoted adherence, to the imams. Tawallī is a set of obligations that a devotee must fulfill towards the imam. In order to better understand this responsibility, let us look at some of the Qur'anic verses and noble traditions addressing our relationship to the imams.

Affection. The Holy Prophet did not ask for any recompense or reward for his delivery of God's message. All he asked of the believers is to abide by his teachings.

قُلْ مَا أَسْأَلُكُمْ عَلَيْهِ مِنْ أَجْرٍ إِلَّا مَن شَاءَ أَن يَتَّخِذَ إِلَىٰ رَبِّهِ سَبِيلًا

Say, 'I do not ask you any reward for it, except that anyone who wishes should take the way to his Lord.'[1]

[1] The Holy Qur'an, 25:57.

The Holy Prophet also asked his ummah to be affectionate towards the people of his household.

قُل لَّا أَسْأَلُكُمْ عَلَيْهِ أَجْرًا إِلَّا الْمَوَدَّةَ فِي الْقُرْبَىٰ ۗ وَمَن يَقْتَرِفْ حَسَنَةً نَّزِدْ لَهُ فِيهَا حُسْنًا

Say, 'I do not ask you any reward for it except affection towards [my] relatives.' Whoever performs a good deed, We shall enhance its goodness for him.[2]

The pairing between affection to the Holy Household and the performance of good deeds is significant. Imam al-Ḥasan said,

اقتراف الحسنة مودتنا أهل البيت

To perform a good deed is to hold affection toward us Ahl al-Bayt.[3]

The Holy Prophet delivered a detailed message with many obligations and prohibitions. Yet affection is the only command that is labeled as an 'ask' and a 'reward' to the Holy Prophet. He did not ask us to be affectionate towards his household simply because of that blood relationship. He instructed us so because it is an integral part of our faith and a way toward our Lord. As the Holy Qur'an states,

قُلْ مَا سَأَلْتُكُم مِّنْ أَجْرٍ فَهُوَ لَكُمْ ۖ إِنْ أَجْرِيَ إِلَّا عَلَى اللَّهِ ۖ وَهُوَ عَلَىٰ كُلِّ شَيْءٍ شَهِيدٌ

Say, 'Whatever reward I may have asked you is for your own good. My [true] reward lies only with Allah, and He is witness to all things.'[4]

The rewards of delivering a divine message are solely with God Almighty. The Holy Prophet asked us to hold dear the members of his household not for his sake, but for our own good. In explaining these noble verses, Imam al-Bāqir said,

الأجر الذي هو المودة في القربى التي لم أسألكم غيرها فهو لكم، تهتدون بها وتسعدون بها، وتنجون من عذاب الله يوم القيامة

The reward of affection – which I asked you for nothing beside it – is for you so that by it you are guided, felicitous, and safeguarded from the punishment of God on the Day of Resurrection.[5]

---

[2] The Holy Qur'an, 42:23.

[3] al-Majlisī, *Biḥār al-anwār*, 23:232.

[4] The Holy Qur'an, 34:47.

[5] al-Rayshahrī, *Ahl al-bayt fī al-kitāb wa al-sunnah*, 361.

Affection towards the Holy Household is a great blessing by which we can attain guidance and the greatest of rewards. We should not belittle this responsibility. Imam al-Ṣādiq said,

لا تستصغروا مودتنا فإنها من الباقيات الصالحات

> *Do not belittle your affection towards us for it is among those righteous deeds that are everlasting.*[6]

We discussed previously the state of faith as either being in a 'temporary lodging' or a 'lasting abode.' As mentioned, devoted adherence to the imams is a means of safeguarding our religion and allowing our hearts to become a lasting abode for our faith. As Imam al-Ṣādiq explained, it is because affection, adherence, and devotion to them are righteous deeds that are everlasting, which will bring us great rewards on the Day of Judgment. As the noble verse states,

وَالْبَاقِيَاتُ الصَّالِحَاتُ خَيْرٌ عِندَ رَبِّكَ ثَوَابًا وَخَيْرٌ مَّرَدًّا

> *Everlasting righteous deeds are better with your Lord in reward, and better at the return [to Allah].*[7]

Thus, affection towards the Holy Household is a significant responsibility and a great asset to be held on Judgement Day.

Love. A great number of narrations focus on the obligation of love, a concept very closely related to affection. Imam al-Ṣādiq said,

إن الرجل ربما يحب الرجل ويبغض ولده فأبى الله عز وجل إلا أن يجعل حبنا مفترضا

> *A man may love a man yet hate his descendants. Thus, God refused to make love for us anything but an obligation.*[8]

The distinction between affection and love is a matter of debate. One opinion holds that love is a high level of affection. This understanding will suffice for the purposes of this book. The point we wish to highlight is the great emphasis that the noble traditions place on this love. For one, love toward the Holy Household is seen as the foundation of faith. Imam al-Ṣādiq said,

لكل شئ أساس وأساس الاسلام حبنا أهل البيت

---

[6] al-Majlisī, *Biḥār al-anwār*, 27:75.

[7] The Holy Qur'an, 19:76.

[8] al-Majlisī, *Biḥār al-anwār*, 23:239.

Everything has a foundation, and the foundation of Islam is love towards us Ahl al-Bayt.[9]

This love is a natural extension of our love to our Lord and His Messenger. The Holy Prophet said,

أحبوا الله لما يغذوكم من نعمه وأحبوني بحب الله وأحبوا أهل بيتي بحبي

Love God for what He showers you with of His blessings. Love me for the love of God. Love the people of my household for my love.[10]

Because of this natural flow of love – as well as their manifestation of His greatest signs – the love of Holy Prophet and his household becomes synonymous to the love of God and the greatest form of worship. Imam al-Ṣādiq said,

من عرف حقنا وأحبنا فقد أحب الله تبارك وتعالى

Whoever knows our right and loves us has loved God Almighty.[11]

إنّ فوق كل عبادةٍ عبادةً ، وحبنا أهل البيت أفضل عبادة

Above every worship there is [a greater form of] worship. Love for us the people of the Household is the best worship.[12]

Adherence. Looking further into the narrations that speak of affection, we find that the Commander of the Faithful said,

العروة الوثقى المودة لآل محمد

The firmest handle is affection towards the household of Muḥammad.[13]

The Holy Qur᾿an commands us to adhere to this firm handle through submission and virtue.

وَمَن يُسْلِمْ وَجْهَهُ إِلَى اللَّهِ وَهُوَ مُحْسِنٌ فَقَدِ اسْتَمْسَكَ بِالْعُرْوَةِ الْوُثْقَىٰ ۗ وَإِلَى اللَّهِ عَاقِبَةُ الْأُمُورِ

Whoever surrenders his heart to Allah and is virtuous, has certainly held fast to the firmest handle, and with Allah lies the outcome of all matters.[14]

---

[9] al-Rayshahrī, *Ahl al-bayt fī al-kitāb wa al-sunnah*, 390.

[10] al-Tirmithī, *al-Jāmi᾿ al-Kabīr*, 6:126.

[11] al-Rayshahrī, *Ahl al-bayt fī al-kitāb wa al-sunnah*, 391.

[12] al-Barqī, *al-Maḥāsin*, 1:247.

[13] al-Rayshahrī, *Ahl al-bayt fī al-kitāb wa al-sunnah*, 359.

[14] The Holy Qur᾿an, 31:22.

In numerous traditions, the Holy Prophet would tell Imam ʿAlī that he and his family are the firmest handle that God spoke of in His holy book. The Holy Prophet would say,

من أحبكم وتمسك بكم فقد تمسك بالعروة الوثقى

> *Whoever loves you and holds fast to you has surely held fast to the firmest handle.*[15]

أنتم حجة الله على خلقه والعروة الوثقى، من تمسك بها اهتدى، ومن تركها ضل

> *You are the proof of God over His creation and the firmest handle, whoever holds fast to it [i.e., the firmest handle] has been guided and whoever forsakes it has deviated.*[16]

Therefore, holding fast and adhering to the imam is an obligation dictated by imamate. If we seek guidance in this world and the best outcomes in the hereafter, we need only adhere to this firmest handle. Otherwise, we risk drowning in the deviation and depravity of this worldly life. Imam ʿAlī said,

من تمسك بنا لحق، من تخلف عنا غرق

> *Whoever holds fast to us has arrived [at salvation], and whoever falls back away from us has drowned.*[17]

Again, the command to adhere to the imams is not arbitrary. It is based on their connection to the divine and their position in proximity to their Lord. Their words and actions are an immaculate manifestation of God's will. To adhere to them is to adhere to the will and commands of God. To adhere to them is to obey their commands and refrain from what they prohibit. The Holy Prophet said,

تمسكوا بطاعة أئمتكم ولا تخالفوهم، فإن طاعتهم طاعة الله، وإن معصيتهم معصية الله

> *Hold fast to obedience of your imams and do not defy them. Surely, obedience to them is obedience to God and disobedience to them is disobedience to God.*[18]

This concept is reflected in the widely known and narrated tradition of *al-thaqalayn*, where the Holy Prophet instructs his followers to hold tight to the Holy Qurʾan and his family. He said,

---

15 al-Rayshahrī, *Ahl al-bayt fī al-kitāb wa al-sunnah*, 363.

16 Ibid, 364.

17 Ibid.

18 al-Rayshahrī, *Ahl al-bayt fī al-kitāb wa al-sunnah*, 363.

إنِّي تارِكٌ فيكم ما إن تمسَّكتُم به لن تضلُّوا بعدي - أحدُهما أعظمُ من الآخَر - كتابُ الله، حبلٌ ممدودٌ من السَّماء إلى الأرض، وعِترتي أهل بيتي، ولن يتفرَّقا حتى يرِدا عليَّ الحوضَ

> *Verily, I am leaving among you that which if you hold firmly to you will never stray after me – one of which is greater than the other – the Book of God, a rope extended from the heavens to the earth, and my kindred ('itrah), my household. Indeed, the two will never separate until they come back to me at the Pond [of al-Kawthar on the Day of Judgment].*[19]

The concept of adherence to the Holy Household is also found in the verses of the Holy Qur'an. The Holy Prophet explained the verse as he was describing Imam 'Alī to a delegation from Yemen,

هو قول الله ﴿إلا بحبل من الله وحبل من الناس﴾، فالحبل من الله كتابه، والحبل من الناس وصيي

> *He is in the words of God, 'except for a rope from God and a rope from the people.'*[20] *The rope from God is His book, and the rope from the people is my viceroy.*[21]

As discussed previously, the proper understanding of the narrations speaking of the complementarity between the Holy Qur'an and the Holy Household is that the two are inseparable. It is not just that they will never disagree or contradict. Rather, one cannot be separated and adhered to without the other. To claim to adhere to one and not the other is an epistemological fallacy. The two must be taken together, and a rejection of one is fundamentally a rejection of both.

Remembrance. As a means of rooting that love and ensuring that adherence, the Holy Household commanded us to always remember them, their teachings, and their tragedies. This remembrance brings us closer to God Almighty, as they are His appointed vicegerents and guides after His Messenger. Thus, to remember them is to grow closer to what God wants of us. Imam al-Bāqir said,

إن ذِكرَنا من ذِكر الله وذِكر عدوِّنا من ذِكر الشيطان

> *Our remembrance is of the remembrance of God. The remembrance of our enemies is of the remembrance of Satan.*[22]

---

[19] al-Tirmithī, *al-Jāmiʿ al-Kabīr*, 6:125.
[20] The Holy Qur'an, 3:112.
[21] al-Nuʿmānī, *al-Ghaybah*, 46.
[22] al-Majlisī, *Biḥār al-anwār*, 72:468.

Remembrance also holds great significance because it ensures the spread of their teachings and the continuity of this school of thought. That is why the imams commanded us to 'revive their cause.' So long as we remember them, we will bring life to their words through implementation of their teachings. Imam al-Ṣādiq said,

رحم الله عبدا اجتمع مع آخر فتذاكرا أمرنا ، فإن ثالثهما ملك يستغفر لهما ،وما اجتمع اثنان على ذكرنا إلا باهى الله تعالى بهما الملائكة، فإذا اجتمعتم فاشتغلوا بالذكر، فإن في اجتماعكم ومذاكرتكم إحياءنا

> *May God have mercy on a servant who meets up with another and remembers our cause. Surely, the third amongst them is an angel seeking forgiveness for them. No two individuals gather for our remembrance except that God Almighty boasts of them to the angels. When you gather engage in remembrance, for your gathering and remembrance bring life to us.*[23]

Reverence. In addition, there are a set of responsibilities outlined in the noble traditions that we can generally categorize as obligations of reverence towards the imams. For one, the Holy Prophet commands us to never step ahead of them but allow them to take their position of leadership.

أهل بيتي نجوم الأرض فلا تتقدموهم، وقدموهم فهم الولاة بعدى

> *My household are the stars of the earth. Do not step ahead of them. Put them forward [as your leaders], for surely they are the guardians after me.*[24]

Moreover, we must always honor these grand individuals and show them great respect. We must celebrate their names and commemorate their lives and actions. The Holy Prophet said,

أيها الناس عظموا أهل بيتي في حياتي ومماتي وأكرموهم وفضلوهم

> *People! Celebrate the people of my household during my life and after my passing, and honor and favor them.*[25]

As leaders of the faith and the faithful community, they provide us with shining examples that we can follow towards our own excellence. They are the guides and immaculate personas that God blessed us with so that

---

[23] al-Rayshahrī, *Ahl al-bayt fī al-kitāb wa al-sunnah*, 382.

[24] al-Majlisī, *Biḥār al-anwār*, 28:201.

[25] Ibid, 36:295.

we can see real examples of obedience, worship, and devotion to Him. The Holy Prophet said,

من سره أن يحيى حياتي، ويموت مماتي ويسكن جنة عدن التي غرسها الله فليوال عليا من بعدي، وليوال وليه، وليقتد بالأئمة من بعدي، فإنهم عترتي ....

Whoever wishes to live as I live, pass as I pass, and live in the Garden of Eden which God planted, then let him adhere to ʿAlī after me and to his devotees. Let him follow the examples of the imams after me, for they are my kindred....[26]

All of these responsibilities fall within the wider umbrella of tawallī. The degree of their correlation and interdependence within that wider concept is an issue which can be studied at length, but which we will not take up for the sake of brevity. More importantly, we now understand that when the noble traditions speak of *wilāya* and tawallī, they are referring to this broader, holistic meaning which encompasses all of these responsibilities.

TABARRĪ

Having understood the meaning of tawallī, we now turn to the concept of tabarrī – dissociation from and repudiation of their enemies. Does it follow from our obligation to be devout adherents of the imams, that we must also repudiate their enemies? Is repudiation a necessary outcome and complement to tawallī? Or are the two concepts distinct and independent?

We have given the example of the independent relationship between prayer and fasting before. Do tawallī and tabarrī hold the same relationship? On the other hand, we have obligations that are interdependent in theory and application. For example, the obligation of belief in God necessitates a rejection of any supposed like or partner to Him. Do tawallī and tabarrī hold a similar interdependent relationship?

Let us first look for answers in the noble traditions. The Commander of the Faithful answered these questions with the following,

لن يحبنا من يحب مبغضنا إن ذلك لا يجتمع في قلب واحد، ما جعل الله لرجل من قلبين يحب بهذا قوما ويحب بالآخر عدوهم.

Whoever loves those who hate us will never love us. The two will never meet in a single heart. God did not create anyone with two

[26] Ibid, 23:139.

hearts so that they may love a group with one heart and love their enemies with the other.[27]

The Imam's words do not just deny that people love the imams and their enemies; they consider it as an impossibility. The love of the Ahl al-Bayt and the love of their enemies cannot be reconciled. Tawallī cannot exist without tabarrī. The Imam continued,

فمن أحب أن يعلم حاله في حبنا فليمتحن قلبه فان وجد فيه حب من ألب علينا فليعلم أن الله عدوه وجبرئيل وميكائيل والله عدو للكافرين.

Whoever wishes to know his state of love for us, let him test his heart. If he finds in it any love to those who incite against us, then let him know that God is his enemy along with Gabriel and Michael. Surely, God is the enemy of the disbelievers.[28]

When a companion of Imam al-Ṣādiq told him that there are those who claim to love both them and their enemies, the Imam responded,

هيهات كذب من ادعى محبتنا ولم يتبرأ من عدونا

Far be it! Whoever claims to love us and does not repudiate our enemies has lied.[29]

In fact, the imams equate love to their enemies to hatred towards them. Imam al-Sajjād relays the following conversation between the Holy Prophet and some of his companions,

قالوا يا رسول الله و كيف نبغضكم بعد ما عرفنا محلكم من الله و منزلتكم، قال (ص): بأن تبغضوا أولياءنا و تحبوا أعداءنا فاستعيذوا بالله من محبة أعدائنا و عداوة أوليائنا فتعاذوا من بغضنا و عداوتنا فإنه من أحب أعداءنا فقد عادانا و نحن منه براء و الله عز و جل منه بريء

They said, 'Messenger of God! How would we scorn you after knowing your stature with God and your position?' He said, 'By scorning our adherents and loving our enemies. Seek refuge in God from the love of our enemies and animosity towards our adherents – you will surely be given refuge from scorn and animosity towards us. Indeed, whoever loves our enemies has scorned

[27] Ibid, 27:83.

[28] Ibid.

[29] Ibid, 27:58.

us. We repudiate him, and God Almighty repudiates him as well.[30]

This concept is not unfamiliar to the Holy Qur᾽an. Numerous holy verses speak about love and scorn for the sake of God. God says,

لَّا تَجِدُ قَوْمًا يُؤْمِنُونَ بِاللَّهِ وَالْيَوْمِ الْآخِرِ يُوَادُّونَ مَنْ حَادَّ اللَّهَ وَرَسُولَهُ وَلَوْ كَانُوا آبَاءَهُمْ أَوْ أَبْنَاءَهُمْ أَوْ إِخْوَانَهُمْ أَوْ عَشِيرَتَهُمْ

You will not find a people believing in Allah and the Last Day endearing those who oppose Allah and His Apostle even though they were their own parents, or children, or brothers, or kinsfolk.[31]

To repudiate and scorn those who opposed, oppressed, and murdered the Ahl al-Bayt is inherent in our love and adherence to them. Our faith in them is not complete without repudiation of their enemies. Imam al-Riḍā said,

كمال الدين ولايتنا والبراءة من عدونا

Perfection of faith is adherence to us and repudiation of our enemies.[32]

What is the reason behind this correlation between tawallī and tabarrī?

The imams are the greatest embodiment of humanity's potential, having achieved the highest levels of excellence and perfection. They are the closest creation to God and are His walking, talking Qur᾽an. This is why they deserve our devout adherence in its full meaning.

There are those who stand on the opposite side of the spectrum, representing the pinnacle of wretchedness and deviance. There is no virtue or merit that is shared by these individuals and the imams. We cannot hold any devotion or adherence toward such individuals because they represent the antithesis of everything that we hold dear.

A similar concept is seen in the belief of tawḥīd. Believing in God means disbelief in any other deity or partner to Him. It means that everything in existence is dependent on Him, while He is the all-independent. Thus, believing in Him dictates that we reject any notion of a being independent from Him. Otherwise, our belief in Him and His attributes would be

---

[30] Ibid, 27:59.

[31] The Holy Qur᾽an, 58:22.

[32] al-Majlisī, *Biḥār al-anwār*, 27:58.

flawed, as we allowed something else to assume a role that is exclusive to Him.

The same applies with tawallī. Being devout adherents of the imams means that we wholeheartedly accept their message and teachings, and that we love and admire them for the love of God. To do so, we cannot allow for our minds to believe what contradicts their teachings, or for our hearts to love those who oppose them and their ideals. Otherwise, we would fall into a contradiction that diminishes the meaning and value of that adherence.

When an individual challenges God and His authority, how can he be loved the same way God is loved? In so far as the person is a symbol of animosity to God and His chosen servants, such an icon of evil loses any love in the hearts of the faithful.

Imagine the scene of Moses splitting the Red Sea and crossing with his followers towards safety. Imagine Pharaoh following with his army, attempting to put an end to God's message. Can anyone truly adhere to both sides, wishing safety and success to both Moses and Pharaoh? If the switch is placed in our hands – giving us the choice to either close the sea and punish Pharaoh for his crimes, or allow him to reach Moses – what would we do? Can we claim to love Moses if we do not press the switch to close the sea? Can we say that we love God and His appointed imams if we do not find it in ourselves to oppose their enemies?

Some might say that they love all creatures and only disapprove of criminal acts. This idea is missing the point we are making here. So far as all creatures are innocent creatures, examples displaying God's magnificence work, they are reminders of God Almighty. They are not icons of evil. But right when we put on the glasses that allow us to see the choices being made by creatures, we begin to see each painting its own colors for which it is morally held accountable.

We begin to see that actions become habits and habits become ingrained traits. A creature that continuously undertakes evil acts becomes an embodiment of evil. While each person is born as a blank slate that is inherently good, an individual who chooses to abuse their freedom begins to personify evil. It is impossible to love the imam and the traitor at once.

The Scope of Tawallī and Tabarrī

Love and adherence should not stop at the Holy Prophet and the Immaculate Imams. It extends further to their followers and devotees. Again, we can draw an analogy here between imamate and tawḥīd. Tawḥīd does not deny the existence of anything other than God. It denies the acknowledgement of any partner to God, but it does not preclude God having creatures who are dependent on Him. Similarly, adherence to the imams also allows room for adherence to others, so long as those others fall within the purview of their guidance.

Our general understanding of tawallī must therefore extend beyond the imams to include their followers. As we often recite in the visitations of the imams,

يا مولاي أنا موال لوليكم، معاد لعدوكم

> *Master, I am an adherent to those who adhere to you and an enemy of your enemies.*[33]

It is not enough to love and adhere to them, but we must also love and adhere to their followers. Tawallī is not just an obligation to be fulfilled, but a formative aspect of our identities. It shapes our identities and our societies in order to create a righteous community geared toward achieving excellence in this world and the next. It creates a faith-based family that the Holy Qur'an and noble traditions gives precedence even over blood-relations in some circumstances.

Imam al-Ṣādiq instructed us to adhere to such individuals and gave us the most shining exemplars from the companions of the Holy Prophet and Imam ʿAlī. He said,

> والولاية للمؤمنين الذين لم يغيروا ولم يبدلوا بعد نبيهم صلى الله عليه وآله واجبة، مثل سلمان الفارسي وأبي ذر الغفاري والمقداد بن الأسود الكندي وعمار بن ياسر و جابر بن عبد الله الأنصاري وحذيفة بن اليمان وأبي الهيثم بن التيهان وسهل بن حنيف وأبي أيوب الأنصاري وعبد الله بن الصامت وعبادة بن الصامت وخزيمة بن ثابت ذي الشهادتين وأبي سعيد الخدري ومن نحا نحوهم وفعل مثل فعلهم والولاية لاتباعهم والمقتدين بهم وبهداهم واجبة

> *Adherence to the believers who did not change or skew after their prophet is obligatory – the likes of Salmān al-Fārisī, Abū Thar al-Ghifārī, al-Miqdād ibn al-Aswad al-Kindī, ʿAmmār ibn Yāsir, Jābir ibn ʿAbdullāh al-Anṣārī, Ḥuthayfah ibn al-Yamān, Abū'l-Haytham ibn al-Tayyihān, Sahl ibn Ḥunayf, Abū Ayyūb al-Anṣārī, ʿAbdullāh ibn al-Ṣāmit, ʿUbādah ibn al-Ṣāmit,*

[33] Ibid, 98:260.

Khuzaymah ibn Thābit of the two testimonies, Abu Sa'īd al-Khidrī, and anyone who was like them and acted as they did. Adherence to their followers and whoever takes them and their example as guidance is obligatory.[34]

The concept of tawallī is not limited to the Immaculate Imams. Similarly, the idea of tabarrī does not mean to repudiate anyone who is not an imam. Repudiation is reserved for those who place themselves in direct opposition to the divine message and its appointed guardians, or who adhere to such individuals. Again, Imam al-Ṣādiq gives us an example of this. He said,

البراءة من أشقى الأولين والآخرين شقيق عاقر ناقة ثمود قاتل أمير المؤمنين عليه السلام واجبة، والبراءة من جميع قتلة أهل البيت عليهم السلام واجبة.

Repudiation of the most wretched of all former and latter generations, the kin of the one who hamstrung the she-camel of Thamūd, the killer of the Commander of the Faithful is obligatory. Repudiation of all those who killed the Ahl al-Bayt is obligatory.[35]

The Holy Prophet and his family defined this scope by aligning the boundary of love and scorn with God's pleasure. Imam al-'Askarī narrates the following conversation between the Holy Prophet and some of his companions,

قال رسول الله صلى الله عليه وآله لبعض أصحابه ذات يوم يا عبد الله أحب في الله وابغض في الله ووال في الله وعاد في الله فإنه لا تنال ولاية الله إلا بذلك

The Messenger of God said to some of his companions one day, 'Servant of God! Love for the sake of God, hate for the sake of God, adhere for the sake of God, and protest for the sake of God. Surely, adherence to God is not attained except through that.

Love for the sake of God is what unites the believers. It is not just a love of God, His Messenger, and the Holy Household, but a love for each other that is built upon one another's proximity to God and effort in seeking His pleasure. This worldview minimizes the significance of bloodline, color, and socioeconomic status. Instead, obedience of God's commands becomes the primary glue that cements the righteous community together. The concept of tawallī is the force of attraction between

---

[34] Ibid, 27:52.

[35] Ibid.

believers. A person will find himself longing to a believer because he characterizes virtue, good manners, obedience to God, and adherence to the appointed guardians of God's faith. These concepts are not alien to one another but rather form the cornerstone of what a good believer should be in the view of our faith.

On the other hand, our scorn should be reserved for individuals who represent the opposite camp – the camp of deviance and disobedience against God's commands. Of course, we must be careful in applying this concept and not expand it beyond its proper scope. There is room for believers to have a legitimate disagreement on issues of faith. Numerous traditions emphasize the need for giving others the benefit of the doubt so that we do not misjudge or hurt anyone. A believer's scorn should be reserved to those whom the Holy Qur'an and noble traditions characterize as the 'imams of misguidance' and their stalwart supporters.

The Holy Prophet continued,

> ولا يجد رجل طعم الايمان وان كثرت صلاته وصيامه حتى يكون كذلك وقد صارت مواخاة الناس يومكم هذا أكثرها في الدنيا، عليها يتوادون وعليها يتباغضون وذلك لا يغني عنهم من الله شيئا

> *'A man will not taste [the sweetness of] belief, even if his prayers and fasts were many, until he becomes like that. However, in this day people's brotherhood has become mostly for the sake of this world –they befriend one another for it and scorn one another over it. That will not avail them against God in any way.'*

The sweetness of belief is not tasted through prayer and fasting. It is through a faith-based connection with the righteous community of believers that we can truly taste the sweetness of faith. This spiritual connection that we have with one another – and that stems from our mutual love of God, the Holy Prophet, the Immaculate Imams, and their adherents – is part and parcel of tawallī.

A companion asked, "How am I to know that I have adhered and protested for the sake of God? Who is the adherent of God so that I may adhere to him? Who is the enemy of God so I may protest him?" Imam al-ʿAskarī said that,

> فأشار له رسول الله صلى الله عليه وآله إلى علي " ع " فقال أترى هذا فقال بلى فقال ولى هذا ولى الله فواله وعدو هذا عدو الله فعاده ثم قال: وال ولى هذا ولو أنه قاتل أبيك وولدك وعاد عدو هذا ولو أنه أبوك وولدك.

The Messenger of God pointed towards ʿAlī and said, 'Do you see this man?' The man replies, 'Yes.' He said, 'The adherent of this man is the adherent of God, so adhere to him. The enemy of this man is the enemy of God, so protest him. Adhere to the adherents of this man even if he were the murderer of your father and your son. Protest the enemy of this man even if he were your father or your son.'[36]

Some people value blood relation over all else. Others see that the greatest value comes from social status and economic class. In many of his actions and traditions, the Holy Prophet attempted to break down this notion to build a community built on faith as the greatest form of social bond. This concept is reflected in multiple verses of the Holy Qurʾan. For example, when relaying the parable of Noah, the Holy Qurʾan tells us that Noah's son had rejected the faith and become an enemy of his father's message. When Noah pleaded with God to save his son from the great flood, God replied,

يَا نُوحُ إِنَّهُ لَيْسَ مِنْ أَهْلِكَ ۖ إِنَّهُ عَمَلٌ غَيْرُ صَالِحٍ

O Noah! Indeed, he is not of your family. Indeed, he is [a personification of] unrighteous conduct.[37]

God did not stop at telling Noah that his son was unrighteous. Instead, He declared that Noah's son was not part of Noah's 'family.' In God's view, adherence to virtue and the divine message are the true bases of a family, and not mere kinship through blood. Due to his rejection of the message and his devious conduct, Noah's son was cast out of his family.

Conversely, an individual can become part of a family out of his acceptance of the message and virtue in conduct. A great exemplar of that is Salmān al-Fārisī, the close companion of the Holy Prophet which is described in the traditions as,

سلمان منا أهل البيت

Salmān is of us Ahl al-Bayt.[38]

Another tradition mentions that a man lamented to Imam al-Ṣādiq about how he and his family, the Banū Umayyah, are doomed to Hellfire. The Imam stopped him and said,

---

36 al-Ṣadūq, *ʿIlal al-sharāʾiʿ*, 1:140.

37 The Holy Qurʾan, 11:46.

38 al-Majlisī, *Biḥār al-anwār*, 10:123.

لست منهم ، أنت أموي منا أهل البيت ، أما سمعت قول الله عز وجل يحكي عن إبراهيم ﴿فمن تبعني فإنه مني﴾ ؟

You are not of them [i.e., Banū Umayyah]. You are an Umayyad from amongst us Ahl al-Bayt. Have you not heard the word of God Almighty recounting that Abraham said, 'whoever follows me indeed belongs to me'? [39]

ʿAṭiyyah al-ʿAwfī narrates that he was with Jābir ibn ʿAbdullāh al-Anṣārī when he visited the graves of Imam al-Ḥusayn and his companions. He says that Jābir looked at the graves and said, "By Him who sent Muḥammad as a messenger with the truth! We have shared with you what you have reaped!" ʿAṭiyyah was confused. He asked Jābir, "How is that the case when we did not ascend a valley, climb a mountain, or strike with a sword, while these people had their heads separated from their bodies, their children were orphaned, and their wives were widowed?" Jābir replied,

سمعت حبيبي رسول الله (ص) يقول: من أحب قوما حشر معهم، ومن أحب عمل القوم أشرك في عملهم

I heard my beloved Messenger of God say, 'Whoever loves a people will be resurrected with them. Whoever loves the action of a people will share in their action.'

Jābir then said, "By Him who sent Muḥammad as a messenger with the truth! My intention and the intention of my companions is the same as that with which al-Ḥusayn and his companions passed!"[40]

The Holy Prophet did not say that if a person loves the action of a people he will share in the 'rewards' of their action. Instead, he said that the person will share in the action itself. A person who loves a community, its values, its morals, and its actions, is a part of that community. His sharing in those actions may not be on the same level as those who sacrificed and performed, but he is still a part of that community. It is a community that is brought together not by time, place, bloodline, wealth, or the like. It is a community built upon faith, values, morals, and conduct.

When we put this in light of our understanding of divine justice, we see that this whole system is created for the sake of humanity. We were

---

[39] al-Mufīd, *al-Ikhtiṣāṣ*, 85; citing: The Holy Qurʾan, 14:36.

[40] al-Majlisī, *Biḥār al-anwār*, 65:131.

commanded to profess the word of 'there is no god but God' not for any value that may go back to God – He is all-sufficient and perfect above any need or benefit. Instead, He commanded us to do so as a grace from Him because doing so is to our benefit and for our wellbeing. Likewise, the crimes that were committed against the prophets and their viceroys were crimes against humanity.

This can bring more clarity to the idea of tabarrī. We scorn those who committed crimes against the Holy Prophet and his household not just because of our love for them. Those crimes were also crimes against each one of us, our families, our communities, and the entirety of humanity. Those crimes did not allow humanity to reap the greatest benefit from God's divine graces and blessings. They prevent us from experiencing God's promise that the earth will be inherited by His righteous servants.

Our discussion of faith as a centerpiece of our worldview, of our responsibilities towards our imams, and of the meanings of tawallī and tabarrī, all showcase the practical repercussions of our conception of imamate. These discussions should be read with that conception in mind, as the theoretical and practical are often intertwined. The reader should contemplate on the concepts and attempt to strengthen their connection to the imam of their time through applying these practical conceptions.

PART III
ADDRESSING MISCONCEPTIONS

ON AUTHORITY

There are those who claim that the quality and scope of authority that we believe the imams hold contradicts with God's absolute power and ability. The claim is that our belief in the imams' creational authority,[1] their witnessing over the actions of creation, their *hidāyah iyṣāliyyah*, and their role as intermediaries of God's grace, all contradict our belief in an omnipotent, self-sufficient God. Thus, they claim that our belief in the imams' extraordinary roles and abilities is a form of fanaticism and disbelief in God Almighty.

To properly address this misconception, we must first recognize that it can be posed in three distinct ways. First, claims are made that it is impossible and inappropriate to say that these abilities are held by anyone but God. Second, there are those who submit that these abilities can be held by the imams but claim that there is no evidence that they did possess such extraordinary powers. Third, a debate can be had as to whether such abilities necessarily follow from their role as imams.

Here, we only wish to dispel the first form of this misconception. We will not delve into the method and degree by which each of these types of authority may be proven. Learned scholars can disagree on this, and this treatise is not meant for us to stake our opinion on the matter. Instead, we wish to address the general misconception that believing in the imams' creational authority creates a theological dilemma. Shia belief in

[1] Creational authority in the imam is the ability and liberty to affect the existence of any being by God's leave. For more, see: al-Khabbāz, *al-Wilāyah al-Takwīniyyah*.

the imams' authority, intercession, and so forth, does not contradict their belief in God's omnipotence and all-perfection.

Counterarguments to Claims of Impossibility

Before we begin posing the counterarguments to this misconception, let us first clarify a rational concept that will help us clear our perception of these issues.

We must acknowledge the Doctrine of Uniformity as a philosophical principle that should guide our rational discourse. Scientists use this doctrine to infer that the laws and theories they deduce about natural phenomena are true regardless of time and place. To restate the doctrine per the words of Muslim philosophers, "all identical things are to be judged equally in terms of what is possible or impossible for them" (*ḥukm al-amthāl fī mā yajūz wa-lā yajūz wāḥid*). In other words, if two things are the same, the same rules and principles should apply to both. If two things are similar in some way, then the same rules apply if those rules are integral to the point of similarity between the two things.

To illustrate let us ask, "Does firewood burn?" The answer is yes. Although we have not tested all pieces of firewood in existence to see if they burn, we can still make a generalization based on inductive reasoning and the Doctrine of Uniformity that firewood is flammable. Let us ask, "Can humans think rationally?" Again, the answer is yes even though there are and might be humans who cannot think rationally because their mental faculties are impaired. The existence of an exception shows that there is a level of detail not considered by the statement. Still, the fact that an exception to the rule applies does not negate the rule but shows a deeper level of complexity.

The problem with many misconceptions is that they do not properly consider the Doctrine of Uniformity. Thus, many of the claims make an attempt to draw a distinction and pass judgment without making a proper and rational distinction. In other words, most of the objections we will face attempt to draw a distinction without a difference.[2]

---

[2] A 'distinction without a difference' is a logical fallacy where one makes an assertion distinguishing between two propositions, but does not provide a real or practical difference by which such a distinction can be made. For example, if someone says, "I did not lie! I intentionally asserted a false statement!" they are making a distinction without a difference.

With this in mind, let us consider some rebuttals to the claim that it is impossible for the imams to hold such powers and abilities.

First, why is there an objection to the concept of their *hidāyah iyṣāliyyah*? This type of guidance acts like a force of spiritual gravity, much like the gravity we experience in the physical world. Our position is that just as there is a force of attraction between physical objects, there is an attraction between souls based on their purity. The soul of an imam holds the greatest spiritual gravity because it is the purest and most tranquil of souls.

Again, keep in mind that we are discussing the possibility of such a relationship. Laying out the evidence in support of this framework comes at a later stage. Addressing the realm of possibility, what is it that would make their *hidāyah iyṣāliyyah* an impossibility?

Second, why is there an objection to our belief that the imam can be part of the world's system of causality? Why is it a problem that the imam can perform extraordinary acts like curing the ill?

The objectors claim that attributing causation to anyone other than God is a form of disbelief and associating a partner to Him. The insufficiency of this claim should be clear to the reader. All around us, we associate causation with different natural phenomena without fear that this association is a form of disbelief. We know that fire causes burning and smoke, yet we cannot reasonably claim that attributing fire as the cause of burning is a form of disbelief or a limit on God's omnipotence.

Throughout history, extraordinary acts were attributed to the imams. The objectors claim that all these came in the form of prayers that God answered, and not as actions undertaken by the imams. This is supposed to solve the problem of attributing causation to the imams – an unfounded solution to a baseless problem. These individuals accept that God's prophets and messengers performed miracles as part of their mission of guidance. Yet they claim it is impossible for the imams to perform extraordinary acts. Again, the objection is based on a distinction without a difference.

There are those who protest, "This extraordinary ability cannot be without God's will to effectuate it!" Our answer to that is, "Of course!" We do not claim that any of the imams' powers and capabilities are independent of God's will. In fact, we believe that all causation falls within the purview of His will and command. A fire would not burn without His will, and the same is true for the powers of the imam.

Third, why is the claim of extraordinary ability a problem, while the claim of extraordinary knowledge is not? God is both omnipotent and omniscient. If a claim of extraordinary ability in a creation is somehow a limit on His omnipotence, then a claim of extraordinary knowledge should also be a limit on His omniscience. Yet all Muslims believe that there existed individuals with extraordinary knowledge throughout time – individuals we call prophets and messengers. What is the distinction between knowledge and ability that would cause one to be a problem and not the other?

Fourth, why are extraordinary abilities attributed to prophets nonproblematic, while the same abilities are problematic when attributed to the imams? Where is the difference between the two? Why can these extraordinary abilities be attributed to angels but not to the imams? Again, these are all distinctions without a difference.

Finally, there are those who believe in the creational authority and other capabilities of the imams but also claim that accepting a broader scope is improper. The claim is that while the prophets and imams have enough authority to perform miracles and other extraordinary acts, this cannot be generalized further. A cap or limit must be placed on their authority or else the power and authority of God is somehow limited.

Again, this claim falls into the fallacy of making a distinction without a difference. If narrow authority is possible and proper, why is general authority a problem? If they can perform miracles, why is intercession a farfetched impossibility? If they can be part of the causal system of the universe, why can they not be the intermediaries of God's grace to His creations?

Some have claimed that we cannot attribute such capabilities and high levels of authority to the prophets and imams because they are mere servants of God. Such a claim confounds the meaning of servitude with deprivation. It understands servitude to God and dependence on Him as absolute poverty and deprivation from wealth, power, authority, and the like. Yet there is no law stating that the highest levels of servitude can only be attained through such poverty. Prophet Solomon was a servant of God but still possessed great power and wealth. On the other side, there are those who look at their poverty and rebel against God due to their view of their position. Thus, there is no real correlation between material deprivation and servitude to God. A true servant of God will realize his dependence and need for the Almighty, but that does not equate with deprivation.

UNDERSTANDING GOD'S INFINITE NATURE

At times, a claim is made that the power and authority we describe as belonging to the prophets and imams cannot be properly attributed. The rationale is that God Almighty's infinite and absolute nature does not allow for any power or authority beside His.

This kind of claim was the foundation for numerous fallacious doctrines and schools of thought. For example, this line of thinking led some to adopt the idea of fatalism. Their claim was that God's absolute knowledge and power does not allow for any sort of free will in human beings. They concluded that all our actions are predetermined, and we therefore have no control over our actions and their outcomes.

To address this misconception, let us consider the following points.

First, if we adopt the idea that God Almighty's infinite nature does not allow for anything other than Him, then we must apply that idea uniformly across the board. If we claim that His infinite power does not allow for any other power, then we must also say that His infinite knowledge does not allow for any other knowledge. We should also hold that His infinite existence does not allow for the existence of anything else. The fact of the matter is we know that we exist. We live in a material world that we know to exist.

Our knowledge of existence will lead us to one of two conclusions: either that the premise is wrong, or that everything in existence is literally Him, and all existences are parts that compose His essence. The latter conclusion is uniformly rejected by Muslims and contradicts the most basic teachings of monotheistic faith. Therefore, the conclusion that we must draw is that the premise is false and there is a way to reconcile between His infinite nature and the finite nature of His creations.

Second, why does this claim arise only when we speak of the extraordinary abilities and authority of the prophets and imams? If God's absolute and infinite power does not allow for power other than His, then this should be applied uniformly. This would mean that no power exists in any creation. This is a restatement of the doctrine of fatalism – another philosophy that the Immaculate Imams rejected and disproved in their traditions.[3] Most individuals who make this claim to reject the extraordinary abilities of the imams do in fact believe in their free will. Their claim is therefore fallacious – it is another distinction without a difference.

Third, our scholars hold that God's infinite nature means that there is no room for another infinite and absolute being. However, it does allow for beings that are finite and within the scope of His absolute power and authority. God's absolute nature means that there can be nothing independent of Him. So long as we recognize a creation's dependence on the Creator, we can resolve the perceived problem raised by this misconception.

We will not discuss this third answer in detail, as it is a delicate and detailed philosophical topic. The reader can find these discussions comprehensively outlined in the works of our scholars.

Suffice it to say that those who accept that natural phenomena can occur by God's will should also accept the possibility of the extraordinary if it is contingent on God's will as well. The entire misconception claiming that attributing extraordinary abilities to the imams is a limit on God's power and ability is built on a misunderstanding of the underlying logical and philosophical principles. If an individual can clarify his understanding of the premises and principles, then the misconception's error becomes clear.

In conclusion, it should be clear that the assumption of extraordinary ability in certain individuals is of the same order as assuming extraordinary knowledge, or even extraordinary personality. There is no rational dilemma with accepting these claims. Therefore, we can rationally accept such abilities and positions as miracles, creational authority, religious authority, witness over the deeds of mankind, and the like. There is no rational issue with these concepts because they are based on an understanding of the extraordinary nature of such individuals who are connected with the divine.

However, the individual must have the correct perception and understanding of the premises and philosophical and logical principles relevant to the discussion – the individual must have a clear understanding of God's power and infinite nature, servitude, the Doctrine of

[3] For example, see: al-Rayshahrī, *Mīzān al-ḥikmah*, 1:363.

Uniformity, and the relationship between knowledge, ability, and truth that we referred to in previous discussions.

Again, in this short treatise we do not intend to go through an exhaustive study of the evidence to prove the truth and existence of these extraordinary abilities in the imams. These studies can be sought in their proper settings. However, we have outlined enough to establish that accepting this understanding of imamate is rationally sound and does not render anyone a heretic or apostate for adopting it.

ON IMMACULACY AND THE HOLY QUR'AN

Another misconception regarding our understanding of imamate stems from an inaccurate reading of the Holy Qur'an.

There are claims made that the general atmosphere established by the Holy Qur'an does not allow for an understanding of immaculacy. In other words, immaculacy is not a Qur'anic concept. Instead, the Holy Qur'an speaks to individuals who we claim to be immaculate with a degree of chastisement. Prophets and messengers, from Adam to our Holy Prophet Muḥammad, are not addressed as immaculate, but as fallible individuals. In the case of Prophet Adam, God says in the Holy Qur'an,

وَعَصَىٰ آدَمُ رَبَّهُ فَغَوَىٰ

Adam disobeyed his Lord and went amiss.[1]

The Holy Qur'an also speaks of the mistakes of our Holy Prophet Muḥammad and how he will be forgiven. The Holy Qur'an says,

إِنَّا فَتَحْنَا لَكَ فَتْحًا مُّبِينًا ۞ لِّيَغْفِرَ لَكَ اللَّهُ مَا تَقَدَّمَ مِن ذَنبِكَ وَمَا تَأَخَّرَ وَيُتِمَّ نِعْمَتَهُ عَلَيْكَ وَيَهْدِيَكَ صِرَاطًا مُّسْتَقِيمًا

Indeed We have inaugurated for you a clear victory, that Allah may forgive you what is past of your sin and what is to come, and

[1] The Holy Qur'an, 20:121.

that He may perfect His blessing upon you and guide you on a straight path.[2]

The same can be said for a number of other prophets and messengers. These and such verses are given as evidence of a general Qur'anic atmosphere that is incompatible with the idea of immaculacy.

There are those who use this argument to deny immaculacy altogether. Others make this claim confessing to the philosophical necessity for immaculacy when it comes to the prophets' and messengers' delivery of their divine messages. However, the claim is that immaculacy cannot be understood with a broader scope than what may be philosophically necessary due to these Qur'anic verses.

Some Guiding Insights

Before delving into the answers to this misconception, let us again delve into some general guiding insights that will assist us in this chapter, as well as in addressing other misconceptions.

Often times, people read the Holy Qur'an and the noble traditions seeking explicit answers that conform to their preconceived notions and biases. We expect the naṣṣ to speak to us in the language of today and spell things out without a hint of ambiguity or metaphor. This expectation is unfounded and unrealistic. The Holy Qur'an was revealed over 1400 years ago, and it spoke to the people of the time in their tongue. Over the past fourteen centuries, much change has occurred on the historical, political, social, and cultural arenas. These changes did not leave language unscathed – the Arabic language also changed with the changes that occurred to the people who spoke it.

Moreover, religious sciences like theology and jurisprudence evolved over the centuries. As the sciences evolved, scholars found it necessary to define certain terms that were not previously defined. This facilitated clearer communication among scholars around their topics of study.

We cannot look to the Holy Qur'an and the noble traditions, expecting them to speak to us in the language of today – with all the changes and all the terms of today. When we seek to understand the concept of immaculacy, we do not need to find it spelled out in those same terms in the Holy Qur'an. Immaculacy is a term that was defined by scholars to

[2] The Holy Qur'an, 48:1-2.

indicate a certain meaning. The term has evolved over time with the evolution of our understanding of the religious sciences.

Thus, when we look to the Holy Qur'an, we should not be looking for the specific term 'immaculacy.' Instead, we must study the Holy Qur'an to see if the meaning and spirit of immaculacy can be found.

It is also not necessary for the Holy Qur'an to speak in the most explicit terms regarding the issue. It may be embedded in the context of the verse. There may even be some verses that create ambiguity due to the literal meaning that they may hold, but which we understand to be vague due to metaphorical or similar reasons.

We must also be cognizant of the power of categorization, as well as its possible disadvantages. When we categorize ideas and study them in detail, we are able to gain a deeper understanding of each. Yet at times, our categorization can also provide some false indications due to the separation it might cause between different concepts. If we study the abilities and authority of the imams in detail and as an independent idea, we may begin to think that God may have delegated the matters of the world to them.[3] However, the error of this idea becomes immediately clear when we combine the idea of their servitude, our understanding of God's absolute independence, and the dependence of all things on Him.

The Holy Qur'an presents these ideas holistically and avoids the pitfalls of categorization. It emphasizes the purity and lofty status of the prophets and imams, while at the same time emphasizing their position as servants of an Almighty Lord. In fact, because deification of holy figures was a rampant problem for previous societies, the Holy Qur'an went to great lengths to emphasize this servitude. Thus, it characterizes God's righteous servants in the verse,

بَلْ عِبَادٌ مُّكْرَمُونَ ۞ لَا يَسْبِقُونَهُ بِالْقَوْلِ وَهُم بِأَمْرِهِ يَعْمَلُونَ

Indeed, they are [His] honored servants. They do not venture to speak ahead of Him, and they act by His command.[4]

[3] The idea of *tafwīḍ* (delegation) is rejected within Shia Islam. In general, the idea postulates that God Almighty created the universe and delegated its matters to the independent management of the Holy Prophet and his family. This idea clearly contradicts our belief in tawḥīd and was explicitly rejected by our immaculate imams. See, for example: al-Majlisī, *Biḥār al-anwār*, 25:328.

[4] The Holy Qur'an, 21:26–27.

Finally, we must keep in mind that the Holy Qur'an uses the great power of parables and metaphors for instructive purposes. Although we believe that the Holy Qur'an should be understood by the plain meaning of its language, we also believe that there are instances where we know that a particular verse is speaking in metaphor. We make this conclusion when other verses, noble traditions, or sound rational principles that point us in that direction.

The best example of this is seen in the verses that seem to personify God and give Him some physical qualities. For example, God says in the Holy Qur'an,

وَلِلَّهِ الْمَشْرِقُ وَالْمَغْرِبُ ۚ فَأَيْنَمَا تُوَلُّوا فَثَمَّ وَجْهُ اللَّهِ ۚ إِنَّ اللَّهَ وَاسِعٌ عَلِيمٌ

> *To Allah belong the east and the west: so whichever way you turn, there is the face of Allah! Allah is indeed all-bounteous, all-knowing.*[5]

Even though the Holy Qur'an specifically mentions the 'face' of God, we believe that He is not bound by the boundaries of place and matter. This is the dictate of sound reason. We reach this conclusion after a detailed study of the holy verses, noble traditions, and precise philosophical discussions. Our scholars unanimously hold that God does not have any material form, despite the existence of verses that seem to indicate the contrary.[6] In such situations, we understand the type of personification attributed to God in the Holy Qur'an as metaphorical – meant to bring a specific idea closer to the human mind despite the limits of our understanding.

Answers

Let us revert to the above stated misconception. Does the Holy Qur'an present an image of God's prophets and messengers that is incompatible with immaculacy?

We will provide three answers to this misconception.

First, let us reflect on Muslim scholars' views of immaculacy. If we look through the opinions of Muslim scholars, we find unanimous agreement on its existence and application in one form or another. The followers of the Holy Household apply it broadly, holding that prophets and imams are immaculate in every action they take from the moment of their birth

---

[5] The Holy Qur'an, 2:115.

[6] Al-Ḥillī, *Kashf al-murād*, 406–9.

to the moment they pass away. Others hold a more restrictive view. They hold that immaculacy is reserved for God's prophets and messengers. Even then, they are not immaculate in all their actions, but only in delivering the message with which they were entrusted.

Even with the disagreement on scope, Muslims agree that immaculacy is necessary and existent to some degree. That leads us to the question, how did such a consensus come about? This question is especially significant when we look at the history of Muslim schools of thought and all of their disagreements. A point of consensus is often hard to find.

The reader should note that consensus[7] is a very complex and rare social phenomena. It does not arise easily. Neither can it withstand the test of time if it were not built on a solid foundation.

There are three possible explanations for why Muslims came to agree on this. It could be that this understanding is the product of humanity's innate, divinely inspired nature and reason. It could be the result of a sound understanding of clear religious texts that leaves no room for ambiguity and disagreement. Or it could be a result imposed by an external force, such as a political authority.

The latter explanation is highly implausible. Political authority was not able to create consensus on any other issue. Even where we know that a government worked to impose a certain doctrine, we find that there are independent voices who provide an opposite perspective. Moreover, why would any political authority seek to impose the idea of immaculacy of prophets and messengers? What political gains would it achieve if its citizens united in accepting this principle? In addition to all this, there is no evidence that an external force – political or otherwise – attempted to impose this doctrine. We must therefore reject this explanation and turn to the other two.

Was this consensus built on mankind's innate, divinely inspired nature and reason? All Muslims believe that the Holy Qur'an does not conflict with mankind's innate nature and reason. If there is anything in it that

---

[7] We are not speaking of consensus in its technical usage within the study of jurisprudence. Consensus in its jurisprudential meaning can be met even when only a handful of scholars agree on an issue, so long as the requisite conditions are met. Neither are we using the term loosely to indicate broad acceptance of the idea. Rather, all Muslims – scholars and laymen from all denominations – unanimously agree that God's prophet's and messengers are immaculate. The unlikeliness of this outcome should not be underestimated.

seems to conflict with reason, we use the context of other verses and the noble traditions to gain a better understanding of what the verse means. This often leads us to conclude that the specific verse is used metaphorically – as is the case with the verses that seem to personify God Almighty.

What does a consensus born out of mankind's innate, divinely inspired nature and reason mean? If this is in fact the source of this consensus, it would contradict the assertion that the Holy Qur'an's verses are incompatible with immaculacy. On the one hand, consensus on the issue would have been shaken by any verse in the Holy Qur'an that alluded to the contrary. On the other hand, any verse that may (when taken at face value) seem to conflict with a rational consensus on immaculacy should be reinterpreted in light of a deeper meaning.

Moreover, if we study other topics that could be approached in a similar way – the idea of free will and predestination, for example – we do not find a similar consensus. If our innate nature and reason was the sole reason behind such consensus, why did it not create a similar consensus on similar issues? This leads us to believe that there was evidence beyond mere reason – evidence rooted in naṣṣ – that helped create consensus on the topic of immaculacy.

Was this consensus built on clear and irrefutable religious evidence? This seems to be the case. As we will see later in this discussion, the Holy Qur'an is replete with evidence that points towards immaculacy.

Let us step back and ask a question. If the Holy Qur'an sets a tone and atmosphere that is incompatible with immaculacy, where did this consensus come from? Would this not create doubt in the minds of Muslim scholars and break this consensus? The fact that this consensus exists should be sufficient to show us that the stated misconception has an erroneous understanding of the cited verses.

Second, keeping in mind that the Holy Qur'an need not specifically state the word 'immaculacy,' we can find many verses that support the concept. The Holy Qur'an highlights certain qualities in God's chosen servants – purity, proximity to Him, certitude, devotion, patience, righteousness, virtue, piety, and many other traits. All these traits used so in such unrestricted senses are incompatible with anything but immaculacy. Let us take a few examples.

In describing Satan's rebellion against God's commands, the Holy Qur'an relays this promise that Satan made,

وَلَأُغْوِيَنَّهُمْ أَجْمَعِينَ ۞ إِلَّا عِبَادَكَ مِنْهُمُ الْمُخْلَصِينَ

> *I will surely pervert them, all except Your dedicated servants among them.*[8]

The reader should note that the verse refers to these servants as *al-mukhlaṣūn* – a meaning that is not adequately reflected in the translation as dedicated. Linguistically, the term *mukhlaṣūn* does not only describe these individuals as dedicated and sincere, but rather there was some divine action and grace that allowed them to reach that status. To better understand the meaning of this term, let us turn to other verses where the word or its derivatives are used. God Almighty says,

كَذَٰلِكَ لِنَصْرِفَ عَنْهُ السُّوءَ وَالْفَحْشَاءَ ۚ إِنَّهُ مِنْ عِبَادِنَا الْمُخْلَصِينَ

> *So it was, that We might turn away from him all evil and indecency. He was indeed one of Our dedicated servants.*[9]

In relaying the story of Prophet Joseph, the Holy Qur'an says that God turned 'all evil and indecency' away from him. God does not describe Joseph as someone who avoided indecency. Rather, the verse described that God repelled evil away from Joseph. This is a clear indication that God selected and purified such individuals. In other verses, God says,

إِنَّا أَخْلَصْنَاهُمْ بِخَالِصَةٍ ذِكْرَى الدَّارِ ۞ وَإِنَّهُمْ عِنْدَنَا لَمِنَ الْمُصْطَفَيْنَ الْأَخْيَارِ

> *Indeed We purified them with exclusive remembrance of the abode [of the Hereafter]. Indeed they are surely with Us among the elect of the best.*[10]

Thus, these individuals who achieved the level of *mukhlaṣūn* were so dedicated and sincere that God Almighty chose them from amongst His servants and purified them so that no evil can reach them. Satan has no authority or ability to pervert these individuals. This is a clear indication of immaculacy from the Holy Qur'an.

Turning to another example, we read in the opening chapter of the Holy Qur'an,

اهْدِنَا الصِّرَاطَ الْمُسْتَقِيمَ ۞ صِرَاطَ الَّذِينَ أَنْعَمْتَ عَلَيْهِمْ غَيْرِ الْمَغْضُوبِ عَلَيْهِمْ وَلَا الضَّالِّينَ

---

[8] The Holy Qur'an, 15:39–40.

[9] The Holy Qur'an, 12:24.

[10] The Holy Qur'an, 38:46–47.

> *Guide us on the straight path, the path of those whom You have blessed — such as have not incurred Your wrath, nor are astray.*[11]

God teaches us to pray to be amongst those whom He blessed and to walk the straight path. Is that a path of sinners and transgressors? Clearly not. Otherwise, why would He have us pray for it? Rather, it is the path of those who obey God's every command. The Holy Qur'an says,

وَمَن يُطِعِ اللَّهَ وَالرَّسُولَ فَأُولَٰئِكَ مَعَ الَّذِينَ أَنْعَمَ اللَّهُ عَلَيْهِم مِّنَ النَّبِيِّينَ وَالصِّدِّيقِينَ وَالشُّهَدَاءِ وَالصَّالِحِينَ ۚ وَحَسُنَ أُولَٰئِكَ رَفِيقًا

> *Whoever obeys Allah and the Apostle—they are with those whom Allah has blessed, including the prophets and the truthful, the martyrs and the righteous, and excellent companions are they!* [12]

When we recite the chapter of *al-Fātiḥah*, we are praying to be amongst those blessed to obey God's commands and walk His straight path – especially His chosen prophets. God commands us to seek the path that the prophets walked. Is He commanding us to walk a path of sin and disobedience? No. It is rather a path of virtue and obedience that we commonly refer to as immaculacy.

Another example is seen in the verse of purification. God says,

إِنَّمَا يُرِيدُ اللَّهُ لِيُذْهِبَ عَنكُمُ الرِّجْسَ أَهْلَ الْبَيْتِ وَيُطَهِّرَكُمْ تَطْهِيرًا

> *Indeed Allah desires to repel all impurity from you, O People of the Household, and purify you with a thorough purification.*[13]

God emphasizes the fact that He wishes to repel evil from the Holy Household. He does not only purify them but purifies them with a thorough purification. This verse is clear in its signification of immaculacy.

Third, in understanding the verses that seem to reproach God's closest servants, we believe that they are a manifestation of their position of servitude to the Almighty – a position which does not contradict their immaculacy in any way.

To understand this point further, we must first recognize that the concept of immaculacy does not mean that all prophets, messengers, and select servants of God are all of one level. There are disparities amongst

---

[11] The Holy Qur'an, 1:6-7.

[12] The Holy Qur'an, 4:69.

[13] The Holy Qur'an, 33:33.

them so that some are greater and closer to God than others. The Holy Qur᾽an is explicit in relaying this meaning when it says,

تِلْكَ الرُّسُلُ فَضَّلْنَا بَعْضَهُمْ عَلَىٰ بَعْضٍ ۘ مِّنْهُم مَّن كَلَّمَ اللَّهُ ۖ وَرَفَعَ بَعْضَهُمْ دَرَجَاتٍ ۚ وَآتَيْنَا عِيسَى ابْنَ مَرْيَمَ الْبَيِّنَاتِ وَأَيَّدْنَاهُ بِرُوحِ الْقُدُسِ

These are the apostles, some of whom We gave an advantage over others: of them are those to whom Allah spoke and some of them He raised in rank, and We gave Jesus, son of Mary, manifest proofs and strengthened him with the Holy Spirit.[14]

Even amongst the closest of God's servants, there are some who reached closer to Him than others. We believe that our beloved Holy Prophet Muḥammad was the one who reached closest to the Almighty – a fact supported by countless traditions.

Although these individuals are immaculate, they arrived at different degrees of proximity to God through their choices and actions. How do immaculate actions lead to differing results? There are instances when more than one viable and permissible choice is available to the individual. A person may take a course of action that is not prohibited, but which is nonetheless not the best course under the circumstances.

For example, a certain case might come before a judge where the guilt of a culprit is proven, but where the law allows the judge discretion in sentencing. Assume that the law allows a sentence of five to ten years for that crime. The defendant is an otherwise law-abiding citizen that poses no harm to society. If the judge sentences the defendant to twenty years, then he has clearly erred. If he sentences the defendant to eight years, he would not be making any error. However, the best action would be to exhibit mercy by giving the defendant the minimum sentence. Sentencing the defendant to five or eight years would both be appropriate, but one is still better than the other.

Going back to the case of immaculate individuals, how do such choices reflect on their relationship with God? Making the better choice will bring the individual closer to his Lord. Making the other choice is still proper, yet it does not allow him to reach his highest potential of excellence. Thus, these individuals look at themselves and see that they have fallen short in some way. Even though they have not sinned, they see

---

[14] The Holy Qur᾽an, 2:253.

that choice as a deficiency and repent to their Lord for their shortcomings.

So how do we understand the verses of the Holy Qur'an where these immaculate individuals are apparently reproached? Although they reached so close to the Almighty, He reproaches them for not drawing even closer.[15]

The Holy Qur'an is the word of God Almighty. It speaks to all of His servants from the perspective of their relationship with Him. We, as individuals of a lower status who are further away from Him, see these individuals as immaculate because they meet the minimum standard of never disobeying His commands. Yet, from their perspective, there is so much more they could have achieved. They believe in a Lord so worthy of worship that nothing they do can ever match His infinite graces. They realize that they can never repay God for His endless blessings and can never give Him the worship that He deserves. In such a relationship, even the most minute shortcoming is worthy of severe chastisement.

Our misconception can be attributed to our misunderstanding of servitude. We think that we can achieve servitude by staying away from what is forbidden and performing our obligations. The fact of the matter is that this constitutes the bare minimum of our responsibility of servitude. There are tiers and levels beyond that which we often neglect and rarely acknowledge or aspire to.

In addition to all this, we must be cognizant of the theological problem most societies faced before and during the time of the revelation of the Holy Qur'an. Those societies often fell into polytheism by believing in and worshiping different deities. They deified individuals of great respect, such as pharaohs and emperors. Even prophets who pleaded with their people to worship God alone were deified during their lives and after their deaths. This should not come as a surprise, as these individuals performed miracles and exhibited the greatest of qualities.

Understanding the revelation within that context allows us to appreciate the great emphasis that the Holy Qur'an places on servitude. Even

---

[15] The same answer applies to the question often asked about the supplications of our Immaculate Imams. Why do they speak to God as if they are wrongdoers? Why do they cry out of fear of His punishment when they did not disobey Him in the least? They do so because even though they reached so close to Him, they reproach themselves for not drawing even closer. It is a reflection of their deep understanding of servitude and dependence – an understanding that we often miss.

when speaking of the prophets and their qualities, the Holy Qur'an does not neglect to mention their position as servants of the Almighty, as shown in the following verses:

> وَوَهَبْنَا لَهُ إِسْحَاقَ وَيَعْقُوبَ ۚ كُلًّا هَدَيْنَا ۚ وَنُوحًا هَدَيْنَا مِن قَبْلُ ۖ وَمِن ذُرِّيَّتِهِ دَاوُودَ وَسُلَيْمَانَ
> وَأَيُّوبَ وَيُوسُفَ وَمُوسَىٰ وَهَارُونَ ۚ وَكَذَٰلِكَ نَجْزِي الْمُحْسِنِينَ ۝ وَزَكَرِيَّا وَيَحْيَىٰ وَعِيسَىٰ
> وَإِلْيَاسَ ۖ كُلٌّ مِّنَ الصَّالِحِينَ ۝ وَإِسْمَاعِيلَ وَالْيَسَعَ وَيُونُسَ وَلُوطًا ۚ وَكُلًّا فَضَّلْنَا عَلَى الْعَالَمِينَ
> ۝ وَمِنْ آبَائِهِمْ وَذُرِّيَّاتِهِمْ وَإِخْوَانِهِمْ ۖ وَاجْتَبَيْنَاهُمْ وَهَدَيْنَاهُمْ إِلَىٰ صِرَاطٍ مُّسْتَقِيمٍ
>
> *And We gave [to Abraham] Isaac and Jacob and guided each of them. And Noah We had guided before, and from his offspring, David and Solomon, Job, Joseph, Moses and Aaron – thus do We reward the virtuous. And Zechariah, John, Jesus and Ilyas – each of them among the righteous. And Ishmael, Elisha, Jonah and Lot – each We graced over all the nations. And from among their fathers, their descendants and brethren – and We chose them and guided them to a straight path.*[16]

The Holy Qur'an describes the great qualities that the prophets possessed – they were virtuous, righteous, guided to the straight path, and privileged over all nations. This praise, along with what we have read before, is indicative of their immaculacy. Still, the Holy Qur'an continues in the very next verse,

> ذَٰلِكَ هُدَى اللَّهِ يَهْدِي بِهِ مَن يَشَاءُ مِنْ عِبَادِهِ ۚ وَلَوْ أَشْرَكُوا لَحَبِطَ عَنْهُم مَّا كَانُوا يَعْمَلُونَ
>
> *That is Allah's guidance: with it, He guides whomever He wishes of His servants. But were they to ascribe any partners [to Allah], what they used to do would not avail them.*[17]

Alongside all the praise, the Holy Qur'an follows up with a description of their role as servants. It does not stop at that word but describes their absolute need and dependence on the Almighty. If they had strayed in the least, all their great work and immense qualities would be for naught.

As we alluded to before, the Holy Qur'an addresses issues in a holistic fashion. God praises the prophets, but with disclaimers describing their servitude to and need for the Almighty. With this, the Holy Qur'an addresses the problem of deification, while at the same time highlighting the great status of His chosen servants.

---

[16] The Holy Qur'an, 6:84–87.

[17] The Holy Qur'an, 6:88.

ON IMMACULACY AND FREE WILL

Shia Muslims believe that God's prophets and messengers, as well as the imams from the progeny of the Holy Prophet are immaculate individuals who do not commit any sin nor neglect any obligation. Immaculacy is attained by these individuals through their free will and by their actions. Moreover, it is a quality that is present in them from the day of their birth to the day they pass away.

How can this quality be both present from birth and attained by free will? If it was attained by choice, then it should not be present in the individual the day they are born. If it is not attained by choice, then it is not much of a praiseworthy quality. Being born into immaculacy would be like being born into royalty – even if it were a higher status, it is not the result of the individual's merit.

To ask a more general question, why were these individuals chosen in the first place? If God chose them for such a high status, what merit is it to them? Did their possession of such qualities come through their personal choice and struggles?

Answer

Before we answer the above questions, we should point out that for the purposes of this treatise we will assume that immaculacy is a trait possessed by God's prophets, messengers, and chosen guardians since their birth. Our scholars have dedicated much time to studying this issue, and the evidence in support of this view can be sought in their works.[1] We will assume this view to be correct as we address the other questions.

Let us first lay out our understanding of how these individuals were chosen for their sublime positions.

We believe that these individuals were not simply chosen by God, but that they chose these positions for themselves. They had the will to attain these high positions and were given them based on their will. They did not simply want it – as you or I might – but they *willed* it. They were not just hoping to attain proximity to their Almighty Lord but were willing to sacrifice for it.

One of the central pillars of our understanding of immaculacy is that it does not conflict with the individual's free will. This topic is discussed in more detail when discussing the immaculacy of God's messengers and prophets. Generally, immaculacy is no virtue if it dictates the individual's actions and behaviors in a way that it infringes on his free will. For the most part, any action taken under duress or without deliberation loses much of its moral significance. If immaculacy meant that the individual is not capable of having an ill thought or partaking in any vice, then the immaculate individual loses his praiseworthy qualities. Moreover, such an individual can no longer serve as a role model to those who do possess free will, as they face challenges and struggles the likes of which he has never experienced.

Therefore, immaculacy is derived through actions taken out of an individual's own free will. A person can gain this quality through his actions and can also lose it through his actions. Immaculacy and all its implications are therefore consistent with the individual's free will. Of course, the reality is that an individual who is endowed with immaculacy and knows its true worth will never let go or act contrary to it. This does not mean that it contradicts the individual's free will in any way. For example, none of us would eat a dead carcass on the side of the road even though we could if we chose to.

We read in the story of Prophet Abraham one of the most beautiful images of this willingness to sacrifice for the sake of God and the rewards that are attained as a result.

---

[1] al-Ḥillī, *al-Bāb al-ḥādī ʿashar*, 38.

قَالَ يَا بُنَيَّ إِنِّي أَرَىٰ فِي الْمَنَامِ أَنِّي أَذْبَحُكَ فَانظُرْ مَاذَا تَرَىٰ ۚ قَالَ يَا أَبَتِ افْعَلْ مَا تُؤْمَرُ ۖ
سَتَجِدُنِي إِن شَاءَ اللَّهُ مِنَ الصَّابِرِينَ ۝ فَلَمَّا أَسْلَمَا وَتَلَّهُ لِلْجَبِينِ ۝ وَنَادَيْنَاهُ أَن يَا إِبْرَاهِيمُ
۝ قَدْ صَدَّقْتَ الرُّؤْيَا ۚ إِنَّا كَذَٰلِكَ نَجْزِي الْمُحْسِنِينَ ۝ إِنَّ هَٰذَا لَهُوَ الْبَلَاءُ الْمُبِينُ ۝
وَفَدَيْنَاهُ بِذِبْحٍ عَظِيمٍ ۝ وَتَرَكْنَا عَلَيْهِ فِي الْآخِرِينَ ۝ سَلَامٌ عَلَىٰ إِبْرَاهِيمَ ۝ كَذَٰلِكَ نَجْزِي
الْمُحْسِنِينَ ۝ إِنَّهُ مِنْ عِبَادِنَا الْمُؤْمِنِينَ

[Abraham] said [to Ishmael], 'My son! I see in dreams that I am sacrificing you. See what you think.' He said, 'Father! Do whatever you have been commanded. If Allah wishes, you will find me to be patient.' So when they had both surrendered [to Allah's will], and he had laid him down on his forehead, We called out to him, 'O Abraham! You have indeed fulfilled your vision! Thus indeed do We reward the virtuous! This was indeed a manifest test.' Then We ransomed him with a great sacrifice, and left for him a good name in posterity: 'Peace be to Abraham!' Thus do We reward the virtuous. He is indeed one of Our faithful servants.[2]

When Abraham passed this 'manifest test,' he was rewarded with the position of imam. God says,

وَإِذِ ابْتَلَىٰ إِبْرَاهِيمَ رَبُّهُ بِكَلِمَاتٍ فَأَتَمَّهُنَّ ۖ قَالَ إِنِّي جَاعِلُكَ لِلنَّاسِ إِمَامًا

When his Lord tested Abraham with certain words and he fulfilled them, He said, 'I am making you an imam of mankind.'[3]

This divine blessing was granted to such individuals when they demonstrated their will to accept and maintain it. The opportunity to attain this blessing was open to everyone. However, we denied ourselves this great benefit by not having the will to carry the weight that comes along with it.

Now let us turn to the initial question – does the fact that these chosen individuals hold such status from birth contradict with the assertion that immaculacy is attained through choice and action? To answer the question, consider the following three points.

First, an omniscient and wise God does not do anything arbitrarily. He does not distinguish between His creatures without a basis. Thus, we cannot assume immaculacy to be arbitrary or baseless. As such, we

---

[2] The Holy Qur'an, 37:102–11.

[3] The Holy Qur'an, 2:124.

conclude that such a divine grant is apportioned between God's servants based on each's will to reach closer and closer to the Almighty.

Second, ascension in these ranks is based on will and free choice. However, there are always limits and context to each choice. Some traits are inherited, and others are learned through a person's childhood environment. Yet an individual does not have any control over such circumstances. On what basis did God create us in such a variety of different contexts?

There are two ways of answering this question. The first is to say that we do not completely understand the basis for God's placing of each individual in a particular atmosphere. We do not know why one individual might be born poor while the other rich. Still, that does not take away the individual's free will. Free will is a topic discussed separately in books of philosophy and theology and is clear in light of human experience. We know that each individual has the ability to make choices, and we have built civilizations and established legal systems based on that understanding. The individual might not be able to control the circumstances of their birth, but that does not affect their free choice on all other matters.

A second way to answer the question is to propose a theoretical understanding of the basis for God's creation of these diverse contexts for each individual. Our understanding is that God provides the best context for each individual to reach whatever it is that they have the will to achieve. If an individual has the will to be a prophet and an imam – as Abraham did – then God will place him in the context and give him the opportunity to reach that level. If an individual wills to be a scholar, then God will create him in the best atmosphere for him to achieve that goal. Thus, the difference in the context of birth and similar circumstances that we see as driven by divine will, is only a reflection of the best atmosphere in which the individual can attain what they have the will to attain.

Third, an infant may be well aware and capable of making choices in ways that we have not yet discovered scientifically-speaking. Prophet Jesus spoke while he was a baby in the cradle. Many of our Imams took on the active Imam role while still very young. It is possible that such noble personalities always made the right choices from the earliest of days, and because God knew that would with His omniscience, He chose to provide them with an additional layer of grace and protection. The purpose of that additional layer of immaculacy is to safeguard those prophets and imams for their roles in guarding the message, commanding the confidence of their people, and being impeccable role models.

Finally, we find that human societies and cultures do not hesitate in valuing and respecting individuals of great talent and skill. All-star athletes are respected and adored for their greatness. This respect, whether we are aware of it or not, reflects an acknowledgement that there is a degree of choice that allowed them to reach that state. We do not respect the greatest athletes simply because they were born with the right physiques. Even though they may have been born with a natural talent, we respect them because we know that it took dedication and perseverance for them to perfect and maintain their abilities.

With such abilities – from immaculacy, to genius, to athletic ability – we respect the individual who perfects and maintains it because we acknowledge that there was a degree of free will and struggle that was necessary.

We do not look down on an individual whose genetics dictated that he would be born with a certain illness. Neither do we respect a person simply because they are born tall. We respect them for how they make use of that gift.

We do not give respect to a specific trait. Respect is gained through a person's struggle and perseverance in achieving a praiseworthy goal. Immaculacy is a trait perfected and maintained through knowledge and righteous work – much different than height or skin color. It is an attribute that is respected and revered due to the merits of its holder and the great trials they persevered.

EPILOGUE

Having understood imamate as a theoretical framework, deciphered our practical responsibility towards it, and addressed some misconceptions surrounding it, we now turn to answer one final question.

Why is imamate necessary in the first place? Rather, why did God send prophets and messengers? Why was it not left up to us – or the gifted and genius amongst us – to put our theoretical and practical reason to work? Why do we need individuals who are human but are extraordinary in every sense? Why do we need immaculacy?

To properly answer the question, we must first properly understand its scope. This line of inquiry can be understood in several different ways.

It can be interpreted as an inquiry into the philosophy of creation. This would mean that the question can be posed about all other aspects of creation. Why is there such diversity in creation? Why did God create mountains and valleys? Why did He create fish and animals? Why did He created such a vast universe filled with galaxies? Such questions are properly answered in the books of theology as part of the discussion on divine justice.

This line of inquiry can also be seen as an examination of God's attributes. Does God's knowledge, power, generosity, and grace dictate that He give us these divinely appointed guides? Again, this question is answered in the books of theology. In short, God Almighty provides to all of existence everything that it has and to the fullest capacity that it can hold. He says,

أَنزَلَ مِنَ السَّمَاءِ مَاءً فَسَالَتْ أَوْدِيَةٌ بِقَدَرِهَا

He sends down water from the sky whereat the valleys are flooded to [the extent of] their capacity.[1]

So long as there are valleys to be filled, His grace dictates that He fills them out of His unending bounties. So long as such individuals – immaculate leaders of humanity – had the capacity and will to fill the roles of prophethood and imamate, His grace dictated that He elevate them to that status.

But why were there creatures with different capacities and wills? This question goes back to the original interpretation of our primary question. Why is there such diversity in creation? Again, the answer to this question can be sought out in the books of theology discussing divine justice.

The third interpretation for our original question – and the one we wish to answer as a final thought in this treatise – looks at human reality and the role of immaculacy within it.

Humanity has several distinctive features that we should consider when we answer this question.

First, we are materialistic beings. We dedicate our lives for the joys and comforts of this transient world. In doing so, we lose sight of the purpose of our creation – to reach excellence in manifesting God's divine attributes through service to Him.

Second, we are animals that are being tugged by their faculties in competing directions. Our appetites drive us to seek wealth and companionship, while our desire for comfort sometimes leads us to laziness. In all of that, we have the capacity to lose sight of purpose and morals. We can start to justify everything we do in terms of our own self-interest.

Third, we have the faculty of reason and the power of choice that distinguish us from other beasts. Theoretical and practical reason allow us to conceptualize and act on ideas such as justice and fairness. Still, our power of choice means that our base faculties can overcome reason and subjugate it to their will.

[1] The Holy Qur'an, 13:17.

We have discussed these distinctive human traits in previous chapters. We saw that they apply to each one of us as individuals, as well as to the collective of human society.

Despite all this, humanity is always looking for meaning. Our innate nature drives us to think about and reach for something higher. Life is a mountain, and we are never content to live at its base. Where is the rope we can hang on to in order to reach higher and higher?

This group – the prophets and imams, mankind's immaculate leaders – are the rope and guide. They provide the guidance and support that allow us to tread safely in our journey up this mountain. Without them, we are left to our own devices to figure out a way up the mountain.

The mountain is not a safe place. The greatest danger is those whose mistakes cause avalanches that threaten to swallow the rest of us. This is especially true in contemporary times, in a world facing grave dangers like climate change and nuclear proliferation. Without the rope and guide, the world is a dismal place.

Still, humanity's hope lies in the fact that there is a rope. There is a guide that is standing ready to lead us onward. All we need to do is put our faith and reliance on them, instead of thinking that we can conquer the mountain by our own devices.

This group, our rope and guide, must therefore be above all criticism. They must be individuals in whom we can put limitless faith. Otherwise, they themselves would need guides and role models. Therefore, it is essential that this group be immaculate. They must possess the particular knowledge that ensures safe passage without a single misstep. They must have the strength and will to overcome their desires and appetites, such that they will not misuse their authority. They must be witness to the actions of their followers so that they can provide them with the best path and correct any of their mistakes. Their *hidāyah īṣāliyyah* gives them a charisma that allows them to effectively lead their followers and draw in those who might not be inclined to follow.

And while we do not have direct access to the last of these guides, we know that they were able to pass along a set of instructions that can help us along this path. They trained their disciples to carry their teachings and legacy. Our scholars and seminarians dedicate their lives to interpreting these instructions and passing them on. All this has given us a way to draw a clear path and achieve balance between our human faculties.

Where would we be without such individuals? Rational people cannot create this balance without such guidance. Humanity attempts to reach this balance through making governments and enacting laws. But even these laws have their basis in divine teachings. So much so that Prophet Moses is seen as one of the earliest lawgivers of humanity. Human reason has led to great advancement for our race, but at great costs. Advances in science and technology have allowed us to lead more comfortable and efficient lives, but at the cost of putting our planet in great jeopardy. We have been able to create laws, governments, and economies that we deem to be fair, only to witness how quickly they can be jeopardized by greed, prejudice, and disinformation.

Humanity needs an immaculate group to provide the crucial guidance needed to ensure balance between reason and the other faculties. Prophets and messengers are humanity's theoretical reason, clarifying the ideas and laying down the law for this balance. Imams are humanity's practical reason, as they deliberate, judge, and lead in accordance with divine dictates. This group of immaculate personalities provides the role model that God, in His infinite grace, set for us to follow. Their possession of that particular knowledge, creational authority, witnessing of our actions, and *al-hidāyah al-iyṣāliyyah* allow them to be properly exercise their role as humanity's collective external reason.

This is the proper conceptualization of imamate that allows us to understand the high status of the imams in our supplications and visitations. As we read in the Grand Comprehensive Visitation,

مَوَالِيَّ لا أُحْصِي ثَنَاءَكُمْ وَ لا أَبْلُغُ مِنَ الْمَدْحِ كُنْهَكُمْ وَ مِنَ الْوَصْفِ قَدْرَكُمْ وَ أَنْتُمْ نُورُ الْأَخْيَارِ
وَ هُدَاةُ الْأَبْرَارِ وَ حُجَجُ الْجَبَّارِ بِكُمْ فَتَحَ اللَّهُ وَ بِكُمْ يَخْتِمُ

> *Masters! I cannot count your merits! I cannot reach your truth with [mere] praise or your excellence with [mere] description! You are the light of the righteous, the guides of the pious, and the proofs of the Supreme [Lord]. With you has Allah began creation and with you He will seal it.*

Their merits are innumerable and their excellence is indescribable. They are the light that guides us towards salvation. Our words cannot praise them enough or show the gratitude that they deserve.

We thank God Almighty for bestowing us with such guides and role models. We ask Him to grant them His greatest bounties in this world and the hereafter, and to count us amongst their followers and servants.

REFERENCED WORKS

Holy Scripture

The Holy Qur'an.

Other Works

al-ʿĀmilī, Muḥammad ibn al-Ḥasan. *Wasāʾil al-shīʿah*. Qum: Muʾassasat Ahl al-Bayt, 1414/1993.

al-Attar, Mariam. *Islamic Ethics: Divine Command Theory in Arabo-Islamic Thought*. London: Routledge, 2010.

al-Balādhurī, Aḥmad ibn Yaḥyā. *Ansāb al-ashrāf*. Beirut: Dār al-Fikr, 1996.

al-Barqī, Aḥmad ibn Muḥammad. *al-Maḥāsin*, gen. ed. Sayyid Mahdī al-Rajāʾī, Qum: al-Majmaʿ al-ʿālamī li-Ahl al-bayt, 2011 CE.

Bell, Daniel. 'Communitarianism'. *The Stanford Encyclopedia of Philosophy* (Fall 2020 Edition), Edward N. Zalta (ed.), https://plato.stanford.edu/archives/fall2020/entries/communitarianism/.

Gaus, Gerald, Shane D. Courtland, and David Schmidtz. 'Liberalism'. *The Stanford Encyclopedia of Philosophy* (Fall 2020 Edition), Edward N. Zalta (ed.), https://plato.stanford.edu/archives/fall2020/entries/liberalism/.

al-Ḥasanī, Hāshim Maʿrūf. *Sīrat al-aʾimmah al-ithnay ʿashar*. Najaf: al-Maktabah al-Ḥaydariyyah.

al-Ḥillī, Jamāl al-Dīn Ibn al-Muṭahhar. *al-Bāb al-ḥādī ʿashar (maʿ sharḥayhi al-Nāfiʿ yawm al-ḥashar wa-Miftāḥ al-bāb)*, ed. Mahdī Muḥaqqiq. Tehran: McGill Institute of Islamic Studies, 1365 Sh/1986.

al-Ḥillī, Jamāl al-Dīn Ibn al-Muṭahhar. *Kashf al-murād fī sharḥ tajrīd al-iʿtiqād*, ed. Ḥasan Ḥasanzādah Āmulī. Rpt. Qum: Mu'assasat al-nashr al-islāmī, 1433/2012.

Hobbes, Thomas. *Leviathan*. London: Penguin Books, 1985.

Ibn ʿAbdulbar, Yūsuf ibn ʿAbdullāh ibn Muḥammad. *al-Istīʿāb fī maʿrifat al-aṣḥāb*. 4 vols. Beirut: Dār al-Jīl.

Ibn ʿAsākir, ʿAlī ibn al-Ḥasan. *Tārīkh dimashq*. Beirut: Dār al-Fikr, 1995.

Ibn Ḥanbal, Aḥmad ibn Muḥammad. *Faḍāʾil al-ṣaḥābah*. Jeddah: Dār al-ʿilm, 1983.

Ibn Khaldūn, ʿAbd al-Raḥmān. *Muqaddimat ibn Khaldūn*. Damascus: Dār Yaʿrub, 2004.

Ibn Ṭayfūr, Aḥmad ibn Abī Ṭāhir. *Balāghat al-nisā'*. Beirut: Dār al-nahḍah al-ḥadīthah, 1972.

al-Juwaynī, Abū'l-Maʿālī. *A Guide to Conclusive Proofs for the Principles of Beliefs [al-Irshād ilā qawāṭiʿ al-adillah]*, tr. Paul Walker. Reading: Garnet Publishing, 2001.

al-Jūzajānī, Ibrāhīm ibn Yaʿqūb. *Aḥwāl al-rijāl*. Faisalabad.

al-Khabbāz, Sayyid Ḍiyāʾ. *al-Wilāyah al-takwīniyyah bayn al-Qur'ān wa'l-burhān*. Qum: Fadak, 2013.

al-Kulaynī, Muḥammad ibn Yaʿqūb. *al-Kāfī*, ed. ʿAlī-Akbar Ghaffārī, 8 vols. Tehran: Dār al-Kutub al-Islāmiyyah, 1388 Sh/2009.

al-Majlisī, Muḥammad Bāqir. *Biḥār al-anwār*. 110 vols. Beirut: Muʿassasat al-Wafāʾ, 1983.

al-Mufīd, Muḥammad ibn al-Nuʿmān. *al-Ikhtiṣāṣ*. Qum: Mu'assasat al-nashr al-islāmī.

al-Nuʿmānī, Muḥammad ibn Ibrāhīm. *al-Ghaybah*, ed. Fāris Ḥassūn. Qum: Anwār al-Hudā, 1422/2001.

al-Qummī, ʿAbbās. *Mafātīḥ al-jinān*. Beirut: Dār al-Aḍwāʾ, 2014.

al-Qummī, Jaʿfar ibn Muḥammad ibn Qawlawayh. *Kāmil al-ziyārāt*. Qum: Muʿassasat al-nashr al-Islāmī, 1417/1996.

al-Raḍī, al-Sharīf Muḥammad ibn al-Ḥusayn. *Nahj al-balāghah*. Beirut: Dār al-Maʿrifah.

al-Rayshahrī, Muḥammad. *Ahl al-bayt fī'l-kitāb wa'l-sunnah*. Qum: Dār al-Ḥadīth, 1375 Sh/1996.

al-Ṣadūq, Muḥammad ibn ʿAlī. *ʿIlal al-sharaʾiʿ*, ed. Sayyid Muḥammad Ṣādiq Baḥr al-ʿulūm. Najaf: al-Maktabah al-Ḥaydariyyah, 1966.

al-Ṣadūq, Muḥammad ibn ʿAlī. *al-Tawḥīd*, ed. Sayyid Hāshim al-Ṭihrānī. Qum: Mu'assasat al-nashr al-islāmī.

al-Ṣadūq, Muḥammad ibn ʿAlī. *Maʿānī al-akhbār*, ed. ʿAlī-Akbar Ghaffārī. Beirut: Dār al-Maʿrifah, 1979.

al-Ṣadūq, Muḥammad ibn ʿAlī. *Man lā yaḍḥuruh al-faqīh*, ed. Sayyid Ḥasan Kharsān. 4 vols. Beirut: Dār al-aḍwāʾ, 1985.

al-Ṭabarī, Muḥammad ibn Jarīr. *Tārīkh al-rusul waʾl-umam waʾl-mulūk [Tārīkh al-Ṭabarī]*, ed. Muḥammad Abūʾl-Faḍl Ibrāhīm, 10 vols. Cairo: Dār al-maʿārif, 1960.

al-Ṭabāṭabāʾī, ʿAllāma Sayyid Muḥammad Ḥusayn. *The Elements of Islamic Metaphysics (Bidayat al-Hikmah)*, tr. Sayyid ʿAli Quli Qarai. 2nd edn. London: ICAS Press, 2018.

al-Ṭabāṭabāʾī, ʿAllāma Sayyid Muḥammad Ḥusayn. *al-Mīzān fī tafsīr al-Qurʾān*. 20 vols. Beirut: Dār al-aḍwāʾ, 1984.

al-Tirmithī, Muḥammad ibn ʿĪsā. *al-Jāmiʿ al-kabīr*. Beirut: Dār al-Gharb al-Islāmī, 1996.

al-Ṭūsī, Muḥammad ibn al-Ḥasan. *al-Amālī*. Qum: Dār al-Thaqāfah, 1414/1993.

al-Wāṣiṭī, ʿAlī ibn Muḥammad. *ʿUyūn al-ḥikam*, ed. Sayyid Ḥusayn Bīrjandī. Qum: Dār al-Ḥadīth, 1376 Sh/1997.

Ibn Kathīr, Ismāʿīl ibn ʿUmar. *al-Bidāyah waʾl-nihāyah*. 14 vols. Beirut: Dār al-kutub al-ʿilmiyyah, 1987.

Ibn Ṭāwūs, ʿAlī ibn Mūsā. *al-Luhūf fī qatlā al-ṭufūf*. Qum: Anwār al-Hudā, 1375 Sh/1996.

Madison, James. *Federalist No. 51*, in *the Federalist Papers*.